POWER BI

for

Finance and Accounting

Unlocking Financial Insights

Kiet Huynh

Table of Contents

CHAPTER I
Introduction to Power BI and Financial Reporting

1.1 Why Choose Power BI for Financial Reporting

The Benefits of Power BI in Financial Reporting

Power BI offers a range of compelling benefits for financial reporting, making it an invaluable tool for finance and accounting professionals. In this section, we'll explore these benefits in detail, providing specific examples and step-by-step instructions where relevant.

1. Data Integration and Accessibility

Power BI allows you to connect to a wide range of data sources, such as accounting software, ERP systems, spreadsheets, and databases. You can seamlessly integrate financial data from different sources into a single report or dashboard. For instance, you can connect to your accounting software to automatically pull in income statements, balance sheets, and transaction data.

Example: Let's say you use QuickBooks for accounting. With Power BI, you can connect to QuickBooks and merge this data with your sales data from a spreadsheet, creating a comprehensive financial report.

2. Interactive Visualizations

Power BI's strength lies in its interactive visualizations. You can create dynamic charts, graphs, and tables that allow users to drill down into financial data with ease. For instance, you can create a bar chart to display monthly revenue, and users can click on a specific month to see the details.

Example: Build an interactive income statement dashboard where users can select different time periods, compare revenue across product categories, and identify top-performing products.

3. Real-time Data Updates

Power BI offers real-time data refresh capabilities. This means your financial reports can automatically update as new data becomes available. For example, if you're tracking daily sales, your dashboard can refresh daily to reflect the latest numbers without manual intervention.

Step-by-Step: To set up automatic data refresh, connect your data source and configure a refresh schedule in Power BI Service, ensuring your financial reports are always up-to-date.

4. Data Modeling and DAX Formulas

Power BI provides a powerful data modeling engine and the Data Analysis Expressions (DAX) language. This allows you to create custom calculations and metrics specific to your financial reporting needs. For instance, you can calculate year-to-date growth, net profit margins, or budget variances using DAX formulas.

Example: Use DAX to calculate the return on investment (ROI) for different projects or product lines, giving you a deeper understanding of financial performance.

5. Collaboration and Sharing

Power BI facilitates collaboration by allowing you to share reports and dashboards with stakeholders. You can control access and permissions, ensuring that the right people have access to the right financial information.

Step-by-Step: Share a financial report with a specific team by publishing it to the Power BI Service and configuring sharing settings.

6. Cost Savings and Efficiency

By automating financial reporting and reducing the time spent on manual data entry and report creation, Power BI can result in significant cost savings and improved efficiency for finance and accounting teams.

Example: Calculate the time and cost savings achieved by automating monthly financial reports in Power BI compared to manual report generation.

In summary, Power BI offers a comprehensive solution for financial reporting, streamlining data integration, visualization, analysis, and collaboration. Its flexibility and efficiency make it an indispensable tool for finance and accounting professionals, providing real-time insights, improving decision-making, and reducing operational costs.

Streamlining Financial Analysis

One of the significant advantages of using Power BI in finance and accounting is its ability to streamline financial analysis. In this section, we'll delve into the specific ways Power BI accomplishes this and provide practical examples and step-by-step instructions.

1. Consolidation of Data Sources

Power BI simplifies financial analysis by consolidating data from various sources into a single, unified platform. This consolidation eliminates the need to manually gather data from multiple systems, reducing the risk of errors and saving valuable time.

Example: Consider a scenario where you have financial data in QuickBooks, Excel spreadsheets, and SQL databases. Power BI allows you to connect to these sources and consolidate them into a single data model for analysis.

2. Automated Data Refresh

Financial analysis often requires up-to-date data. Power BI enables automated data refresh, ensuring that your reports and dashboards are always current. This automation minimizes the time spent on manual data updates.

Step-by-Step: Set up a scheduled data refresh in Power BI to automatically update your financial reports at regular intervals, such as daily or weekly.

3. Advanced Calculations and Metrics

Power BI's Data Analysis Expressions (DAX) language empowers financial analysts to create complex calculations and metrics with ease. DAX allows you to calculate financial ratios, growth rates, and performance indicators specific to your business.

Example: Use DAX to calculate the debt-to-equity ratio, return on assets, or working capital turnover, providing deeper insights into financial performance.

4. Interactive Visualizations for Drill-Down Analysis

Power BI's interactive visualizations enable finance professionals to perform drill-down analysis effortlessly. You can create hierarchical reports that allow you to explore financial data from a high-level overview to detailed insights with a few clicks.

Example: Build an interactive income statement dashboard that allows you to drill down from the company-wide view to specific department or product-level details.

5. Scenario Analysis and What-If Analysis

Power BI supports scenario analysis, allowing you to assess the impact of different financial scenarios on your organization. This feature is invaluable for making informed decisions based on various assumptions.

Step-by-Step: Create a What-If parameter in Power BI to explore the financial implications of changing variables like sales growth rate or cost reductions.

6. Collaboration and Sharing

Streamlining financial analysis extends to collaboration. With Power BI, you can share reports and dashboards with colleagues and decision-makers. Collaboration becomes seamless as stakeholders access the same data for discussions and decision-making.

Step-by-Step: Share a financial analysis report with your finance team by publishing it to the Power BI Service and granting access to team members.

In summary, Power BI streamlines financial analysis by consolidating data sources, automating data updates, facilitating advanced calculations, and promoting collaboration. These capabilities enhance the efficiency of financial analysts and empower data-driven decision-making, ultimately saving time and improving financial insights.

Empowering Informed Decision-Making

Empowering informed decision-making is a critical aspect of utilizing Power BI in finance and accounting. In this section, we'll explore how Power BI facilitates data-driven decisions, providing practical examples and step-by-step instructions where relevant.

1. Real-Time Insights

Power BI's ability to provide real-time insights empowers decision-makers with up-to-the-minute information. This real-time data access allows finance and accounting professionals to make timely decisions based on the most current financial data.

Example: Imagine you're monitoring your company's daily sales trends. With Power BI, you can access real-time sales data and identify potential issues or opportunities as they happen.

2. Interactive Dashboards for Exploration

Power BI's interactive dashboards allow decision-makers to explore financial data in a user-friendly manner. Users can interact with the data, drill down into details, and filter information, enabling deeper exploration.

Example: Create an interactive dashboard for executive leadership that visualizes key performance indicators (KPIs) and allows them to filter data by time period, department, or region for a comprehensive view of the company's financial health.

3. Customized Reporting

Power BI enables the creation of customized reports tailored to the specific needs of decision-makers. These reports can include only the relevant information, ensuring that decision-makers focus on the critical factors.

Step-by-Step: Design a customized financial report for the CFO that highlights key financial metrics, budget variances, and trends specific to their decision-making requirements.

4. Scenario Analysis for Risk Mitigation

Power BI's ability to perform scenario analysis helps decision-makers assess the potential impact of different financial scenarios. This feature is crucial for risk mitigation and strategic planning.

Step-by-Step: Create multiple scenarios to explore the financial outcomes of various decisions or external factors (e.g., market conditions) and evaluate their impact on the organization.

5. Collaboration and Sharing

Decision-makers can collaborate effectively using Power BI. By sharing reports and dashboards, they ensure that the entire team has access to the same data, facilitating discussions and alignment on financial decisions.

Step-by-Step: Share a decision-oriented financial report with a cross-functional team, allowing them to collaborate and provide input within the report.

6. Data-Backed Strategy Formulation

Power BI's insights help in the formulation of data-backed strategies. Decision-makers can use financial data to devise strategies for growth, cost reduction, or optimization, enhancing the organization's competitiveness.

Example: Leverage Power BI to identify underperforming product lines and formulate a strategy to either improve their performance or phase them out to increase overall profitability.

7. Data-Driven Compliance and Risk Management

Power BI supports decision-makers in ensuring compliance and managing financial risks. By monitoring key compliance metrics and risk factors, organizations can proactively address potential issues.

Example: Create a risk management dashboard that highlights critical financial compliance metrics, allowing decision-makers to take immediate action when thresholds are breached.

In summary, Power BI empowers informed decision-making by providing real-time insights, interactive dashboards, customized reporting, scenario analysis, collaboration, data-backed strategy formulation, and data-driven compliance and risk management. This enables finance and accounting professionals to make more informed, timely, and strategic decisions based on reliable financial data.

1.2 Getting Started with Power BI

Introduction to Power BI

Power BI is a robust business intelligence tool developed by Microsoft, designed to help finance and accounting professionals unlock the power of data visualization and data-driven decision-making. In this section, we'll provide a comprehensive introduction to Power BI, covering its core features and how it can be used effectively in the finance and accounting field.

What is Power BI?

Power BI is a suite of business analytics tools that allows you to connect to various data sources, transform and model data, and create interactive, visually appealing reports and dashboards. It offers a seamless way to turn raw financial data into valuable insights and share them with stakeholders.

Key Features of Power BI for Finance and Accounting:

1. Data Connectivity:

   - Power BI can connect to a wide range of data sources, including databases, spreadsheets, cloud services, and on-premises data.

   - Example: Connect Power BI to your accounting software, such as QuickBooks or Excel, to extract financial data.

2. Data Transformation and Modeling:

   - You can clean, shape, and transform your financial data using Power BI's Power Query Editor.

- Create data models that define relationships between different data tables for accurate analysis.

- Example: Cleanse and structure financial transaction data to eliminate errors and inconsistencies.

3. Data Visualization:

  - Power BI offers a rich library of visualizations, including charts, graphs, and tables.

  - Interactive visualizations allow you to explore financial data, making it easier to identify trends and anomalies.

  - Example: Create a bar chart to visualize monthly revenue, or a slicer to filter data by date or product category.

4. DAX Formulas:

  - The Data Analysis Expressions (DAX) language in Power BI allows you to create custom calculations and measures.

  - Perform complex financial calculations, such as calculating compound interest or forecasting revenue growth.

  - Example: Use DAX to calculate year-over-year growth in sales or compute the net present value (NPV) of an investment.

5. Data Refresh and Automation:

  - Schedule data refreshes to keep your reports up to date.

  - Automate report generation and distribution to save time and ensure data accuracy.

  - Example: Set up a daily data refresh to automatically update daily sales reports.

6. Sharing and Collaboration:

  - Publish reports to the Power BI service for easy sharing and collaboration.

- Control access to reports, dashboards, and datasets to ensure data security.

- Example: Share a financial dashboard with your team, granting specific access to each member.

Getting Started with Power BI:

1. Installation and Setup:

  - Download and install Power BI Desktop, the free desktop application for report creation.

  - Sign in to your Power BI account or create one if you don't have it.

  - Example: Go to the Power BI website, download the Desktop application, and create a Power BI account.

2. User Interface Overview:

  - Familiarize yourself with Power BI Desktop's user interface, including the fields pane, report view, and data view.

  - Learn how to import data, create visuals, and design reports.

  - Example: Open Power BI Desktop, connect to a sample dataset, and create a simple bar chart.

3. Data Import and Transformation:

  - Explore data import options, including importing from files, databases, and online services.

  - Use Power Query Editor to clean and transform data for analysis.

  - Example: Import a CSV file with financial data, clean the data to remove duplicates, and create a data model.

4. Creating Visuals and Reports:

  - Build your first financial report using Power BI's drag-and-drop interface.

- Choose appropriate visuals, apply filters, and format your report for clarity.

- Example: Create a report that visualizes monthly revenue, expenses, and profit, and add a slicer for date filtering.

In summary, Power BI is a powerful tool for finance and accounting professionals, offering a wide array of features for data connectivity, transformation, visualization, and automation. This introduction provides a solid foundation for getting started with Power BI and harnessing its capabilities to unlock financial insights.

The Power of Data Visualization in Finance

Effective data visualization is a cornerstone of financial analysis, and Power BI offers a powerful platform for transforming raw financial data into insightful visualizations. In this section, we will explore the significance of data visualization in finance, its advantages, and how to leverage Power BI to create compelling visualizations.

Why Data Visualization Matters in Finance:

1. Enhanced Comprehension:

  - Data visualization makes complex financial data more accessible and easier to understand.

  - Visuals like charts and graphs provide a clear and concise representation of trends, patterns, and outliers in financial data.

  Example: Visualize quarterly revenue growth over several years with a line chart, making it easier to identify fluctuations and trends.

2. Quick Decision-Making:

  - Visualizations enable faster decision-making by presenting information at a glance.

- Finance professionals can quickly spot issues or opportunities in financial data, facilitating timely responses.

Example: A well-designed dashboard can show real-time sales performance, allowing for immediate decisions on inventory management or marketing strategies.

3. Effective Communication:

   - Visualizations are a universal language that transcends data literacy barriers.

   - They facilitate better communication of financial insights to stakeholders, making it easier to convey the significance of the data.

Example: Present a financial report to non-financial stakeholders using visualizations to explain revenue sources, cost breakdowns, and profit margins.

4. Pattern Recognition:

   - Visualizations help in identifying patterns, correlations, and anomalies in financial data that might be overlooked in raw numbers.

   - Heatmaps, scatter plots, and trendlines are valuable for discovering hidden insights.

Example: Create a scatter plot to analyze the relationship between marketing expenditure and sales, identifying areas where increased spending leads to higher revenue.

5. Data Comparison:

   - Visualizations allow for effective comparison of financial data across different periods, products, or business units.

   - Comparisons help in making informed decisions based on historical data and performance.

Example: Use a bar chart to compare monthly expenses for different departments, highlighting areas where cost reductions can be made.

Leveraging Power BI for Data Visualization in Finance:

1. Selecting the Right Visuals:

   - Power BI offers a wide range of visualizations, including bar charts, line charts, pie charts, and more.

   - Choose visuals that best represent your financial data and the insights you want to convey.

   Step-by-Step: When creating a report in Power BI, select appropriate visuals that enhance the understanding of your data, such as using a stacked column chart for expense breakdowns.

2. Interactive Visuals:

   - Power BI allows you to create interactive visuals that enable users to explore data by interacting with the report.

   - Use slicers, drill-through, and cross-filtering to make your visuals interactive.

   Step-by-Step: Implement slicers in your report that enable users to filter data by time period, product category, or other relevant dimensions.

3. Customizing Visuals:

   - Customize the appearance of visuals to improve clarity and relevance.

   - Adjust colors, labels, and data labels to make your visualizations more informative.

   Step-by-Step: Modify the colors and data labels on a pie chart to highlight the percentage of expenses in each category.

4. DAX Calculations for Advanced Visuals:

- Utilize DAX (Data Analysis Expressions) to create custom calculations for advanced visuals.

- Perform calculations like year-over-year growth rates, running totals, or financial ratios.

Example: Write DAX formulas to calculate the average annual growth rate of revenue and display it in a card visual.

5. Effective Dashboard Design:

- Organize your visuals into interactive dashboards that tell a coherent financial story.

- Arrange visuals in a logical flow that guides users through key insights.

Step-by-Step: Design a financial dashboard that starts with an executive summary and allows users to explore detailed financial metrics through interactive visuals.

In summary, data visualization is a powerful tool in finance, enabling better understanding, quicker decision-making, and effective communication of financial insights. Power BI's extensive capabilities in data visualization make it a valuable asset for finance and accounting professionals, helping them create impactful visuals that drive informed decisions and enhance financial reporting.

Installing Power BI and Initial Setup

1.2.3. Installing Power BI and Initial Setup

Installing Power BI and setting it up correctly is the first step to harnessing its powerful capabilities for financial reporting. In this section, we will guide you through the process of downloading, installing, and performing the initial setup of Power BI.

Step 1: Download Power BI Desktop

1. Visit the official Power BI website (https://powerbi.microsoft.com/) and navigate to the "Products" section.

2. Select "Power BI Desktop" and click on the "Download free" button.

3. Choose the version that matches your operating system (Windows 64-bit or 32-bit).

4. Click "Download" to start downloading the installation file.

Step 2: Installation

1. Locate the downloaded installation file (usually in your "Downloads" folder) and double-click it to begin the installation.

2. Follow the on-screen prompts to install Power BI Desktop on your computer.

3. Accept the license terms and select your preferred installation location.

4. Click "Install" to start the installation process.

5. Wait for the installation to complete. It may take a few minutes.

Step 3: Launching Power BI Desktop

1. Once the installation is complete, you can launch Power BI Desktop.

2. Look for the Power BI Desktop icon on your desktop or search for "Power BI Desktop" in the Windows Start menu.

3. Double-click the icon to open the application.

Step 4: Initial Setup

1. When you first launch Power BI Desktop, you may be prompted to sign in with your Microsoft account. If you don't have a Microsoft account, you can create one at this stage.

2. Signing in is not mandatory for using Power BI Desktop, but it allows you to access additional features like publishing reports to the Power BI service.

3. If you choose to sign in, enter your Microsoft account credentials and follow the sign-in process.

Step 5: User Interface Overview

1. Familiarize yourself with the Power BI Desktop user interface. It consists of several key components, including the following:

   - Fields Pane: This is where you manage data sources and fields.

   - Report View: This is where you design and view your reports and visuals.

   - Data View: This is where you can see your data and apply transformations.

Step 6: Connect to Data Source

1. Start by connecting Power BI to your data source. Click on "Get Data" or "Home" on the ribbon to access various data source options.

2. Select the data source you want to connect to (e.g., Excel, SQL database, or web service).

3. Follow the prompts to connect to your data source and load the data into Power BI Desktop.

Step 7: Data Transformation

1. Use Power Query Editor to clean, shape, and transform your data as needed.

2. Apply filters, remove duplicates, and perform other data preparation tasks to ensure the data is ready for analysis.

Step 8: Creating Visuals

1. After loading and transforming your data, you can start creating visualizations.

2. Drag and drop fields from the Fields Pane onto the report canvas to create visuals like charts, tables, and maps.

Step 9: Saving Your Work

1. Save your report by clicking "File" and then "Save" or "Save As."

2. Choose a location on your computer to save the Power BI file.

Step 10: Publish to Power BI Service (Optional)

1. If you want to share your reports with others, you can publish them to the Power BI Service.

2. Click "Publish" and follow the prompts to upload your report.

Conclusion:

Installing Power BI and performing the initial setup is the foundation for your journey to unlocking financial insights. With Power BI Desktop installed and configured, you can begin connecting to data sources, creating visualizations, and generating valuable financial reports.

1.3 Understanding Finance and Financial Reporting

Fundamentals of Finance

Understanding the fundamentals of finance is essential for effective financial reporting with Power BI. In this section, we will delve into the core concepts of finance, providing a solid foundation for financial analysis and reporting.

Key Finance Fundamentals:

1. Time Value of Money (TVM):

 - TVM is a fundamental concept that emphasizes the idea that money today is worth more than the same amount of money in the future.

 - It is crucial for financial professionals to understand TVM when calculating present value, future value, and interest rates.

 Example: Calculate the future value of a $1,000 investment at a 5% annual interest rate after 5 years using the TVM formula.

2. Financial Statements:

 - Financial statements are the backbone of financial reporting and analysis.

 - There are three primary financial statements: the balance sheet, the income statement, and the cash flow statement, each serving a unique purpose.

 Example: Explain the purpose of a balance sheet in summarizing a company's financial position at a specific point in time.

3. Financial Ratios:

   - Financial ratios are tools used to evaluate a company's financial health and performance.

   - Key ratios include liquidity ratios, profitability ratios, and leverage ratios, among others.

   Example: Calculate the current ratio for a company using its current assets and current liabilities and interpret the result.

4. Risk and Return:

   - The risk-return trade-off is a core concept in finance, suggesting that higher returns typically come with higher risk.

   - Finance professionals must consider risk when making investment decisions or assessing the performance of financial assets.

   Example: Compare the expected returns and risk levels of two different investment portfolios to demonstrate the risk-return trade-off.

5. Discounted Cash Flow (DCF):

   - DCF analysis is used to determine the present value of future cash flows.

   - It plays a crucial role in valuing investments, projects, and business opportunities.

   Example: Use DCF analysis to calculate the present value of cash flows for a potential investment and determine whether it's a financially sound decision.

Leveraging Power BI for Finance Fundamentals:

1. Data Import and Transformation:

- Use Power BI to import and transform financial data from various sources, including accounting software and databases.

- Cleanse data to ensure accuracy and consistency, and prepare it for financial analysis.

Step-by-Step: Import financial data from an Excel spreadsheet, identify and address data inconsistencies or errors using Power Query, and load the clean data into Power BI.

2. Creating Financial Visualizations:

- Utilize Power BI's visualization capabilities to create visuals that represent financial concepts and data.

- Design financial dashboards that provide a visual summary of key financial metrics.

Step-by-Step: Create a dashboard that includes visuals like bar charts for profitability ratios, line charts for revenue trends, and cards displaying key financial figures.

3. Data Analysis and Calculation:

- Leverage Power BI's DAX functions to perform financial calculations and analyses.

- Calculate financial ratios, perform TVM calculations, and apply DCF analysis within Power BI.

Example: Write a DAX formula to calculate the return on investment (ROI) for a specific project using cash flows and initial investment data.

4. Data Presentation and Reporting:

- Design financial reports that effectively communicate financial insights and analysis.

- Arrange visuals and tables in a way that conveys financial information clearly to stakeholders.

Step-by-Step: Create a financial report in Power BI that includes an executive summary, financial statements, and detailed analyses, and use the report layout features for clarity.

5. Interactive Reporting:

   - Implement interactivity in your financial reports using Power BI's features like slicers and drill-through.

   - Allow users to explore financial data, change perspectives, and gain insights interactively.

Step-by-Step: Add slicers to your financial report that enable users to filter financial data by date range, product category, or other dimensions for dynamic analysis.

In summary, understanding the fundamentals of finance is crucial for effective financial reporting with Power BI. This section provides you with the foundational knowledge needed to apply finance concepts within the Power BI environment, enhancing your ability to create insightful financial reports and analyses.

The Significance of Financial Reports

Financial reports are the lifeblood of any organization, providing a comprehensive view of its financial health and performance. In this section, we will explore the significance of financial reports, their role in decision-making, and how Power BI can be harnessed to create meaningful financial reports.

Importance of Financial Reports:

1. Performance Evaluation:

   - Financial reports, such as income statements and balance sheets, are vital tools for evaluating a company's financial performance over a specific period.

- They provide insights into revenue, expenses, assets, liabilities, and equity, allowing stakeholders to assess profitability and financial stability.

Example: Analyze an income statement to determine whether a company achieved its revenue and profit targets for a quarter.

2. Investor Confidence:

  - Accurate and transparent financial reports instill confidence in investors and creditors.

  - Investors rely on financial reports to make informed decisions about allocating capital.

Example: Investors review a company's financial reports to assess its financial health before purchasing its stock or bonds.

3. Regulatory Compliance:

  - Many organizations are legally required to produce and publish financial reports, ensuring compliance with accounting and financial regulations.

  - These reports often adhere to established accounting standards, such as Generally Accepted Accounting Principles (GAAP) or International Financial Reporting Standards (IFRS).

Example: A publicly traded company must file quarterly and annual reports with the Securities and Exchange Commission (SEC) in the United States.

4. Strategic Decision-Making:

  - Financial reports serve as a foundation for strategic decision-making within an organization.

  - Executives and management use these reports to set budgets, plan investments, and make operational decisions.

Example: A company's board of directors uses financial reports to decide whether to invest in expanding its production capacity.

5. Comparative Analysis:

- Financial reports enable comparative analysis by presenting historical data and allowing stakeholders to assess changes over time.

- This helps identify trends, patterns, and areas that require attention or improvement.

Example: Compare revenue and expenses from the current year to the previous year to identify growth or cost reduction opportunities.

Creating Meaningful Financial Reports with Power BI:

1. Data Integration:

- Use Power BI to integrate data from various sources, including accounting software, databases, and spreadsheets.

- Combine data from multiple departments or systems to create comprehensive financial reports.

Step-by-Step: Connect Power BI to your organization's financial data sources and combine data into a single dataset for reporting.

2. Data Transformation and Cleansing:

- Employ Power Query in Power BI to transform and cleanse financial data.

- Cleanse data by removing duplicates, addressing inconsistencies, and structuring it for reporting.

Example: Use Power Query to remove duplicate entries in a ledger and ensure that financial data is accurate.

3. Financial Calculations:

- Utilize Power BI's DAX functions to perform financial calculations and create custom measures.

- Calculate key financial ratios, such as profitability margins, return on investment, and liquidity ratios.

Example: Write DAX measures to calculate the gross profit margin and return on assets (ROA) for your organization.

4. Visual Storytelling:

- Leverage Power BI's visualization capabilities to create visual reports that tell a clear financial story.

- Design interactive dashboards with visuals like charts, graphs, and tables.

Step-by-Step: Create a financial dashboard in Power BI that visualizes key financial metrics, such as revenue trends, expense breakdowns, and net profit over time.

5. Automation and Updates:

- Schedule data refreshes in Power BI to keep your financial reports up-to-date.

- Automate report generation and distribution to save time and ensure timely access to financial insights.

Step-by-Step: Set up a scheduled data refresh in Power BI to ensure that your reports always reflect the latest financial data.

In summary, financial reports are crucial for assessing an organization's financial health, making informed decisions, and complying with regulatory requirements. Power BI empowers finance and accounting professionals to create meaningful financial reports by integrating, transforming, and visualizing data effectively, allowing stakeholders to gain valuable insights for decision-making and strategic planning.

Organizing Financial Data

Effectively organizing financial data is a crucial step in the process of creating meaningful financial reports with Power BI. In this section, we will explore the best practices for structuring and organizing financial data for optimal analysis and reporting.

Best Practices for Organizing Financial Data:

1. Data Structure:

  - Establish a well-defined structure for your financial data. This typically involves organizing data into tables or spreadsheets with clear column headings.

  - Ensure that each row of data represents a unique financial transaction or entity.

  Example: Create a structured Excel spreadsheet with separate sheets for income statements, balance sheets, and cash flow statements, with consistent column headers.

2. Consistency and Standardization:

  - Maintain consistency in data formatting and naming conventions. Standardize currency symbols, date formats, and units of measurement.

  - Ensure that data is consistently labeled and categorized for accurate analysis.

  Example: Use the same currency symbol (e.g., USD) across all financial data, and ensure that dates are consistently formatted as MM/DD/YYYY.

3. Data Validation and Cleansing:

- Before importing data into Power BI, validate and cleanse the data to eliminate errors, duplicates, and inconsistencies.

- Check for missing data points and resolve them to ensure the completeness of your financial dataset.

Step-by-Step: Use data validation techniques in Excel or Power Query to identify and address data errors and inconsistencies.

4. Data Relationships:

- Establish relationships between different financial data tables. For example, connect income statements, balance sheets, and cash flow statements using common identifiers.

- Ensure that relationships are set up correctly to enable cross-table analysis.

Example: Link transaction data to customer data using a unique customer ID, allowing you to analyze customer-specific financial performance.

5. Hierarchical Data:

- If your financial data has a hierarchical structure, such as multiple levels of accounts or cost centers, ensure that the hierarchy is clearly defined.

- Create parent-child relationships between data elements to enable hierarchical reporting and analysis.

Example: Organize expense categories hierarchically, where higher-level categories (e.g., "Operating Expenses") roll up into more specific subcategories (e.g., "Marketing Expenses").

Leveraging Power BI for Data Organization:

1. Data Import and Transformation:

- Utilize Power BI's data import capabilities to bring structured financial data into the application.

- Power Query in Power BI allows for advanced data transformation and cleansing.

Step-by-Step: Import structured financial data from Excel or other sources into Power BI, using Power Query to perform necessary data transformations.

2. Data Modeling:

- Create a logical data model within Power BI by defining relationships between tables.

- Utilize the Model view to manage relationships, hierarchies, and calculated columns.

Example: Define relationships between financial data tables, such as connecting income statements to corresponding balance sheets using common identifiers.

3. Calculated Columns and Measures:

- Use Power BI's DAX (Data Analysis Expressions) language to create calculated columns and measures.

- Calculated columns can be used to generate additional data points, while measures are used to perform calculations on the fly.

Step-by-Step: Write DAX expressions to create calculated columns that compute key financial ratios, and measures that calculate year-to-date performance.

4. Data Hierarchies:

- Utilize Power BI's hierarchy features to organize hierarchical data for efficient analysis.

- Create hierarchies that allow users to drill down from high-level summaries to detailed data.

Example: Establish a product hierarchy that allows users to navigate from product categories to individual products in financial reports.

5. Data Refresh and Scheduling:

   - Set up scheduled data refreshes in Power BI to keep your financial reports up-to-date.

   - Automate the process to ensure that new financial data is regularly incorporated.

Step-by-Step: Configure scheduled data refresh in Power BI to maintain the accuracy and timeliness of your financial reports.

In summary, organizing financial data is a critical component of effective financial reporting with Power BI. By following best practices and leveraging Power BI's data transformation and modeling capabilities, finance and accounting professionals can create well-structured datasets that facilitate meaningful analysis and reporting.

1.4 Power BI for Financial Analysis

Leveraging Power BI for Financial Insights

Power BI is a powerful tool for finance and accounting professionals, offering the capability to unlock valuable financial insights. In this section, we'll explore how to leverage Power BI to gain meaningful financial insights and provide step-by-step guidance on the process.

Key Benefits of Leveraging Power BI for Financial Insights:

1. Data Integration:

 - Powcr BI cnables the integration of financial data from various sources into a unified platform.

 - Combine data from accounting software, spreadsheets, databases, and other sources to create a comprehensive financial view.

 Step-by-Step: Import data from multiple sources into Power BI, including data cleansing and transformation steps where needed.

2. Data Visualization:

 - Create interactive and visually compelling financial reports and dashboards using Power BI's extensive visualization capabilities.

 - Choose from a wide range of visual elements, including charts, tables, maps, and more.

 Step-by-Step: Design financial dashboards in Power BI by selecting appropriate visuals and arranging them to convey financial insights effectively.

3. Real-Time Reporting:

   - Power BI allows for real-time or scheduled data updates, ensuring that financial reports are always up-to-date.

   - Users can access the latest financial information without manual data entry or updates.

   Step-by-Step: Configure data refresh schedules in Power BI to maintain the currency of financial reports.

4. Interactivity and Drill-Through:

   - Enable interactivity in financial reports, allowing users to explore data, change perspectives, and gain deeper insights.

   - Implement drill-through functionality for a detailed view of financial data.

   Step-by-Step: Add interactive features like slicers and drill-through options to financial reports to enhance user experience.

5. Advanced Calculations:

   - Utilize DAX (Data Analysis Expressions) in Power BI to perform advanced financial calculations and create custom measures.

   - Calculate financial ratios, perform time value of money (TVM) calculations, and analyze profitability.

   Example: Write DAX expressions to calculate key financial metrics like return on investment (ROI), net present value (NPV), or debt-to-equity ratio.

6. Hierarchical Data Analysis:

   - Analyze hierarchical financial data by creating hierarchies and enabling drill-down analysis.

- Explore financial data from high-level summaries to detailed breakdowns for better decision-making.

Example: Create hierarchies for product categories, allowing users to drill down from product groups to individual product details in financial reports.

Steps to Leverage Power BI for Financial Insights:

1. Data Source Connection:

- Connect Power BI to your financial data sources, which may include accounting software, databases, and spreadsheets.

- Choose the appropriate data connection method based on your source.

Step-by-Step: Use Power BI's data source connectors to establish connections with your financial data sources.

2. Data Transformation:

- Utilize Power Query in Power BI to transform and cleanse data, addressing inconsistencies, missing values, and data errors.

- Prepare data for analysis by structuring it according to your reporting needs.

Step-by-Step: Apply data transformation techniques using Power Query to ensure data accuracy and consistency.

3. Data Modeling:

- Create a logical data model in Power BI, defining relationships between data tables and hierarchies.

- Ensure that the model reflects the structure of your financial data accurately.

Example: Define relationships between tables such as income statements, balance sheets, and cash flow statements, and create hierarchies where needed.

4. Visual Report Design:

- Design financial reports and dashboards in Power BI, selecting appropriate visuals for your key financial metrics.

- Create reports that offer a clear and insightful view of your organization's financial performance.

Step-by-Step: Utilize Power BI's visualizations to create meaningful financial reports, arranging visuals and providing interactivity.

5. Calculation and Analysis:

- Use DAX functions in Power BI to perform financial calculations and analyses.

- Calculate financial ratios, analyze time series data, and gain insights into financial performance.

Step-by-Step: Write DAX expressions for advanced calculations and analyses that align with your financial reporting objectives.

6. Sharing and Collaboration:

- Share financial reports and dashboards with stakeholders within your organization.

- Collaborate with team members, enabling them to access and interact with the financial data.

Step-by-Step: Publish and share financial reports through Power BI's sharing and collaboration features, ensuring secure access.

In conclusion, Power BI is a valuable tool for finance and accounting professionals, offering the capability to unlock valuable financial insights. By leveraging Power BI's data integration, visualization, real-time reporting, interactivity, advanced calculations, and hierarchical analysis, you can create comprehensive and meaningful financial reports that drive informed decision-making and enhance financial performance.

Benefits of Using Power BI in Finance

Power BI offers numerous advantages for finance professionals, enabling them to make data-driven decisions and unlock valuable insights. In this section, we will explore the specific benefits of using Power BI in finance and provide practical examples to illustrate these advantages.

Key Benefits of Using Power BI in Finance:

1. Data Integration and Consolidation:

   - *Benefit:* Power BI allows finance teams to consolidate data from various financial sources, such as accounting software, spreadsheets, and databases.

   - *Example:* A finance department can integrate financial data from multiple branches or divisions to create consolidated financial reports, simplifying overall analysis.

2. Real-Time Reporting:

   - *Benefit:* Power BI supports real-time data updates, ensuring that financial reports always reflect the latest information.

   - *Example:* Finance professionals can track key financial metrics, such as daily sales revenue or expenses, in real-time dashboards.

3. Data Visualization:

   - *Benefit:* Power BI's extensive visualization capabilities enable finance professionals to create visually compelling and interactive financial reports and dashboards.

   - *Example:* Visualizations like line charts, pie charts, and maps help finance teams convey financial insights effectively.

4. Interactivity and Drill-Through:

   - *Benefit:* Power BI provides interactivity features, allowing users to drill down into financial data for a deeper understanding.

   - *Example:* A CFO can drill through a high-level financial summary to access detailed transaction data for a specific time period.

5. Advanced Calculations and Analysis:

   - *Benefit:* Power BI's DAX (Data Analysis Expressions) language enables finance professionals to perform advanced financial calculations and analyze data.

   - *Example:* Finance teams can calculate complex financial metrics, such as compound annual growth rate (CAGR) or discounted cash flow (DCF) analysis.

6. Automated Reporting:

   - *Benefit:* Power BI allows finance professionals to automate report generation and distribution, saving time and ensuring regular access to financial insights.

   - *Example:* Finance departments can schedule daily, weekly, or monthly financial reports for executives or team members.

7. Hierarchical Data Analysis:

   - *Benefit:* Power BI supports hierarchical data analysis, helping finance professionals explore financial data from high-level summaries to detailed breakdowns.

- *Example:* Finance professionals can navigate through a product hierarchy to analyze sales performance at different levels of product categories.

8. Cost Savings:

   - *Benefit:* Power BI can reduce costs associated with manual data entry and reporting, as well as minimize the need for extensive IT support.

   - *Example:* An organization can save time and resources by automating previously manual reporting processes.

9. Collaboration and Sharing:

   - *Benefit:* Power BI enables finance teams to share financial reports and collaborate with colleagues within the organization.

   - *Example:* Finance professionals can share interactive dashboards with team members, enabling collaborative data analysis.

Practical Implementation of Power BI Benefits in Finance:

1. Data Integration and Consolidation:

   - *Implementation:* Finance professionals can use Power BI to connect to multiple data sources, create relationships between tables, and consolidate financial data for in-depth analysis.

2. Real-Time Reporting:

   - *Implementation:* Finance teams can set up scheduled data refreshes in Power BI to ensure that financial reports remain up-to-date.

3. Data Visualization:

- *Implementation:* Utilize Power BI's drag-and-drop visualizations to design financial reports with meaningful charts, graphs, and tables.

4. Interactivity and Drill-Through:

  - *Implementation:* Add slicers, filters, and drill-through options to financial reports to enhance user interaction and exploration.

5. Advanced Calculations and Analysis:

  - *Implementation:* Leverage DAX expressions to perform financial calculations, such as calculating ROI or NPV, and create custom measures for deeper analysis.

6. Automated Reporting:

  - *Implementation:* Configure scheduled data refreshes and automate report generation in Power BI for timely access to financial insights.

7. Hierarchical Data Analysis:

  - *Implementation:* Create hierarchies in Power BI to explore hierarchical financial data and enable drill-down analysis.

8. Cost Savings:

  - *Implementation:* Calculate the time and resource savings achieved by automating manual reporting processes using Power BI.

9. Collaboration and Sharing:

  - *Implementation:* Use Power BI's sharing and collaboration features to distribute financial reports and enable team members to collaborate effectively.

In conclusion, Power BI offers significant benefits for finance professionals, including data integration, real-time reporting, data visualization, interactivity, advanced analysis, automation, hierarchical data exploration, cost savings, and collaboration. By implementing these benefits in practical finance scenarios, organizations can make data-driven decisions and gain valuable financial insights that drive improved financial performance and decision-making.

Setting up Your Financial Data Sources

Setting up your financial data sources is a crucial step in leveraging Power BI for financial analysis and reporting. In this section, we'll delve into the process of preparing, connecting, and structuring your financial data sources for effective use in Power BI, including specific examples and practical guidance.

Steps to Set Up Your Financial Data Sources in Power BI:

1. Identify Data Sources:

 - Begin by identifying the sources of your financial data. These sources may include accounting software, ERP systems, spreadsheets, databases, and external data providers.

 - List the data sources you need to connect to Power BI for comprehensive financial reporting.

 Example: Your data sources might include QuickBooks for transaction data, Excel spreadsheets for budget information, and an SQL database for historical financial records.

2. Data Extraction:

 - Extract data from your identified sources. Depending on the source, this may involve exporting data to a common format like CSV or connecting directly to databases.

 - Ensure that the data extraction process preserves the integrity of the original data.

Step-by-Step: Export financial data from QuickBooks to CSV files and use SQL queries to extract relevant data from the SQL database.

3. Data Cleaning and Transformation:

- Prior to importing data into Power BI, perform data cleaning and transformation. This involves addressing issues like missing values, data inconsistencies, and formatting errors.

- Ensure that the data is clean, structured, and ready for analysis.

Step-by-Step: Use Power Query in Power BI to clean and transform data, addressing issues such as removing duplicates, standardizing date formats, and handling missing values.

4. Data Integration:

- Combine data from multiple sources if necessary. Power BI provides tools to merge and append data from various files or databases.

- Establish relationships between different datasets to enable cross-source analysis.

Step-by-Step: Merge financial data from Excel spreadsheets with transaction data from QuickBooks and establish relationships between the datasets.

5. Data Modeling:

- Create a logical data model within Power BI by defining relationships between tables. Ensure that the model reflects the structure of your financial data.

- Consider creating calculated tables and columns for additional insights.

Example: Define relationships between tables for income statements, balance sheets, and cash flow statements, and create calculated columns for financial ratios.

6. Data Source Connection:

- Use Power BI's data source connectors to connect to your financial data. Power BI supports various connectors, such as Excel, SQL Server, SharePoint, and many cloud-based data sources.

- Configure data source connection settings, including authentication and access permissions.

Step-by-Step: Connect Power BI to your SQL Server database, specifying the server details, authentication method, and database selection.

7. Scheduled Data Refresh:

- Configure scheduled data refresh in Power BI to ensure that your financial reports are regularly updated with the latest data.

- Set appropriate refresh frequencies based on the data source.

Step-by-Step: Schedule daily data refresh for transaction data from QuickBooks and weekly refresh for budget data from Excel spreadsheets.

8. Data Security and Permissions:

- Define data security and permissions to control access to financial data within Power BI. Implement role-based security if necessary.

- Ensure that only authorized users can access sensitive financial information.

Example: Limit access to confidential financial data to the finance team and executives while providing broader access to less sensitive financial reports.

9. Testing and Validation:

- Before deploying financial reports, thoroughly test and validate the data connections and refresh schedules.

- Verify that data is accurately imported and refreshed as expected.

Step-by-Step: Perform test imports and data refreshes, comparing the results with the original data sources to confirm accuracy.

10. Documentation:

- Maintain documentation of data source connections, data transformation steps, and refresh schedules for reference and auditing purposes.

- Document any issues and solutions encountered during the setup process.

Example: Create a data source documentation file that includes connection details, transformation steps, and refresh schedules for future reference.

By following these steps, you can effectively set up your financial data sources in Power BI, ensuring that your data is clean, structured, and ready for analysis. This foundation is crucial for generating meaningful financial reports and unlocking valuable insights to support financial decision-making within your organization.

CHAPTER II
Exploring Power BI for Financial Reporting

2.1 Importing and Transforming Financial Data

Importing Financial Data into Power BI

One of the initial steps in leveraging Power BI for financial reporting is importing financial data into the Power BI platform. This process involves connecting to your data sources, selecting the appropriate tables or files, and configuring data import settings. In this section, we'll provide a comprehensive guide on how to import financial data into Power BI, with practical examples and detailed steps.

Steps to Import Financial Data into Power BI:

1. Launch Power BI Desktop:

   - Start by opening Power BI Desktop, the application that allows you to create and manage financial reports.

2. Access the Home Tab:

   - In Power BI Desktop, go to the "Home" tab, which is your starting point for data import and transformation.

3. Select Data Source:

- Click on the "Get Data" option on the "Home" tab. A dropdown menu will appear with various data source options.

Example: Choose "Database" if your financial data source is a database, or select "Excel" if your data is in an Excel workbook.

4. Connect to Data Source:

- Depending on your choice of data source, you'll be prompted to provide connection details. For databases, this includes server information and credentials. For Excel, you'll browse to the file location.

Step-by-Step: If connecting to a database, enter the server details and login credentials. If using an Excel file, navigate to the file location and select the appropriate sheet.

5. Data Navigator:

- After connecting to the data source, the "Navigator" window will appear. This window displays a list of tables, views, or sheets available in your data source.

Example: In the case of an Excel workbook, you'll see a list of sheets. Choose the one containing your financial data.

6. Select Data Tables:

- In the "Navigator" window, select the specific data tables or sheets that contain your financial data. You can preview the data by clicking on a table.

Example: If your financial data is in an Excel sheet named "Sales," select this sheet for import.

7. Load Data:

- After selecting the desired tables, click the "Load" button. Power BI will import the selected data into your report.

8. Data Transformation:

- Depending on the complexity of your financial data, you may need to perform data transformation steps. This can include cleaning data, removing unnecessary columns, and renaming columns.

Step-by-Step: Click on "Edit Queries" to access the Power Query Editor, where you can perform data transformation steps.

9. Data Preview:

- Once your data is loaded, you can preview it in the "Fields" pane on the right-hand side of the Power BI Desktop interface.

Example: The "Fields" pane will display a list of columns from the imported financial tables.

10. Data Relationships:

- If your financial data includes multiple tables with related information, you'll need to establish data relationships within Power BI. This enables cross-table analysis.

Step-by-Step: Go to the "Model" view in Power BI to define relationships between tables using primary and foreign keys.

11. Scheduled Refresh:

- Configure scheduled data refresh settings to ensure that your financial data is updated regularly in Power BI.

Step-by-Step: In the Power BI Service, set up data refresh schedules according to your data source update frequency.

By following these steps, you can successfully import your financial data into Power BI, making it ready for analysis and reporting. Power BI's intuitive interface and data import capabilities make this process accessible to both finance professionals and data analysts, providing a strong foundation for creating insightful financial reports.

Cleaning and Transforming Financial Data

Once you've imported financial data into Power BI, the next crucial step is cleaning and transforming that data to make it suitable for analysis and reporting. Financial data often comes with inconsistencies, missing values, and the need for specific calculations. In this section, we'll explore the process of cleaning and transforming financial data in Power BI, providing practical examples and detailed steps.

Steps to Clean and Transform Financial Data in Power BI:

1. Access Power Query Editor:

   - Click on the "Edit Queries" button to open the Power Query Editor, a powerful tool in Power BI for data cleaning and transformation.

2. Review Data Source:

   - In the Power Query Editor, you'll see a preview of the data you've imported. Take a moment to review the structure and content of your financial data.

3. Handling Missing Values:

- Identify and handle missing values in your financial data. You can remove rows with missing values or replace them with appropriate values.

Example: If a financial dataset contains missing values in the "Revenue" column, you can replace them with zeros or interpolate missing values.

4. Column Renaming:

- Rename columns to make them more descriptive and user-friendly. Clear, well-named columns enhance the clarity of your data.

Step-by-Step: Right-click on a column header and select "Rename" to give it a meaningful name, like changing "Col1" to "Transaction Date."

5. Column Formatting:

- Format columns to match the data type they represent. For instance, dates should be formatted as date types, and numbers as currency or percentages.

Example: Ensure that date columns are formatted as dates, and monetary values as currency.

6. Removing Unnecessary Columns:

- Eliminate any columns that aren't relevant to your analysis or reporting. Reducing clutter in your data model can improve performance.

Step-by-Step: Select the columns you want to remove and click "Remove Columns" in the Power Query Editor.

7. Data Type Conversion:

   - Convert data types when necessary. For instance, you may need to change text columns to numbers for calculations.

   Example: Convert text-based "Quantity" columns to whole numbers for mathematical operations.

8. Data Sorting:

   - Sort data in a logical order, such as by date or numerical value, to make it easier to analyze.

   Step-by-Step: Use the sorting options in Power Query to arrange data columns in the desired order.

9. Data Filtering:

   - Apply filters to exclude unwanted data. This can involve removing outliers, selecting specific time periods, or focusing on certain categories.

   Example: Filter the data to include only the last year's financial records.

10. Calculated Columns:

   - Create calculated columns to derive new insights or perform calculations that aren't available in the original data.

   Step-by-Step: Use Power Query functions to create calculated columns, such as calculating profit margins or year-over-year growth.

11. Data Preview and Validation:

- Regularly preview your data in the Power Query Editor to ensure that your cleaning and transformation steps are accurate and meet your data quality standards.

12. Data Load:

- After cleaning and transforming your financial data in the Power Query Editor, load the data back into Power BI by clicking the "Close & Apply" button.

By following these steps, you can effectively clean and transform your financial data in Power BI, ensuring that it is ready for meaningful analysis and reporting. This process plays a crucial role in ensuring the accuracy and reliability of your financial insights, empowering informed decision-making within your organization.

Managing Data Relationships

Effective data relationships are key to harnessing the full power of Power BI for financial reporting. In this section, we'll explore how to manage data relationships in Power BI, with a focus on creating, configuring, and maintaining relationships between tables in your financial data model. We'll provide practical examples and detailed steps to guide you through the process.

Steps to Manage Data Relationships in Power BI:

1. Open the Power BI Model:

- Launch Power BI Desktop and open the financial report or model you're working on.

2. View Relationships:

- Go to the "Model" view in Power BI, where you can visualize and manage data relationships between tables.

3. Identify Tables:

- Examine the tables in your financial model and determine which tables need to be related to one another. Typically, tables with common fields, like transaction IDs or dates, are good candidates for relationships.

Example: You may have tables for transactions, products, and customers that should be related based on common fields like "TransactionID" and "CustomerID."

4. Create Relationships:

- To create a relationship, drag and drop a field from one table to a matching field in another table. Power BI will automatically detect the relationship type (one-to-one, one-to-many, or many-to-one) based on the data.

Step-by-Step: Drag the "CustomerID" field from the "Transactions" table to the "CustomerID" field in the "Customers" table to create a one-to-many relationship.

5. Configure Relationships:

- Configure relationship options as needed. You can specify filtering direction, cross-filtering behavior, and active or inactive status for each relationship.

Example: You might configure a relationship to allow bi-directional filtering, where filtering one table filters related data in the other table.

6. Check Data Model:

- Review the data model diagram in Power BI to ensure that your relationships are correctly represented.

7. Test Relationships:

- Perform testing to confirm that your relationships are working as expected. Use slicers and filters to see how changes in one table affect data in related tables.

Step-by-Step: Apply a filter to a date field in the "Transactions" table and observe how it filters data in the "Products" and "Customers" tables.

8. Maintain Relationships:

- Regularly review and maintain your data relationships as your financial model evolves. Ensure that new tables or fields are appropriately related to existing data.

Example: When introducing a new "Suppliers" table, create relationships with existing tables like "Transactions" and "Products."

9. Complex Relationships:

- In some cases, you may need to handle complex relationships, such as many-to-many relationships. Power BI provides tools for managing such scenarios.

Step-by-Step: For a many-to-many relationship between "Products" and "Transactions," use a bridge table that connects both tables.

10. DAX Measures:

- Create Data Analysis Expressions (DAX) measures to perform calculations that involve related tables. DAX is a powerful language for creating custom calculations.

Example: Use DAX to calculate revenue per customer based on transaction data and customer information.

11. Data Validation:

- Regularly validate your financial reports to ensure that data relationships are functioning correctly. Compare results with the original data sources.

Step-by-Step: Use DAX measures to calculate financial metrics, such as profit margins, and compare them with external financial reports.

12. Documentation:

- Maintain documentation of your data relationships, including diagrams and descriptions, for reference and auditing purposes.

Example: Create a data model documentation file that includes diagrams of data relationships and their configurations.

By following these steps, you can effectively manage data relationships in Power BI, enabling you to perform in-depth financial analysis and create insightful financial reports. Properly configured relationships allow you to slice and dice financial data to gain valuable insights and make informed financial decisions within your organization.

2.2 Building Basic Financial Reports

Creating Cash Flow Statements

Cash flow statements are essential financial reports that provide insights into a company's liquidity and financial health. In this section, we'll guide you through the process of creating cash flow statements in Power BI. We'll cover the necessary steps, data sources, calculations, and visualizations to build a comprehensive cash flow statement report.

Steps to Create Cash Flow Statements in Power BI:

1. Data Sources:

 - Identify the data sources required to create a cash flow statement. Common data sources include financial transaction records, accounts payable and receivable, and other financial data.

 Example: You may use tables containing cash transactions, accounts payable, and accounts receivable data.

2. Data Transformation:

 - Ensure that your financial data is cleaned, transformed, and properly structured. This may involve aggregating transactions, handling data formatting, and handling missing values.

 Step-by-Step: Use Power Query in Power BI to perform data transformation and cleaning, as described in earlier sections.

3. Calculations:

 - Calculate the various components of a cash flow statement, including operating cash flows, investing cash flows, and financing cash flows. These calculations often involve subtracting cash outflows from cash inflows.

 Example: Calculate operating cash flows by subtracting operating expenses from cash revenues.

4. Cash Flow Categories:

 - Group cash flows into categories, such as operating, investing, and financing activities. Define measures for each category to organize your data.

Step-by-Step: Use DAX (Data Analysis Expressions) to create measures that sum cash flows within each category.

5. Time Period Selection:

- Allow users to select the time period for the cash flow statement, such as monthly, quarterly, or annually. Implement slicers or filters to facilitate this selection.

Example: Create a slicer that enables users to choose the financial reporting period.

6. Visualizations:

- Design visualizations for your cash flow statement report. Consider using tables, charts, and graphs to represent different sections of the statement.

Step-by-Step: Add visual elements to your report by using Power BI's visualizations and custom formatting options.

7. Cash Flow Statement Structure:

- Create a clear and structured layout for the cash flow statement, including sections for operating, investing, and financing activities. Use text boxes and labels for clarity.

Example: Design a report layout with headers for each section, followed by tables or charts for cash flows.

8. Interactive Features:

- Implement interactive features to enhance user experience. Users should be able to click on data points for additional details or navigate through different time periods.

Step-by-Step: Use Power BI's interactive features like drill-through or bookmarks to enable user interaction.

9. Data Validation:

- Validate the accuracy of your cash flow statement by comparing it to external financial reports or other reliable sources. Ensure that the calculated cash flows align with accounting standards.

Example: Compare the cash flow statement results in Power BI with the statement generated by your accounting system.

10. Documentation:

- Document the data sources, calculations, and report structure for future reference and auditing.

Step-by-Step: Create documentation that explains the data sources, DAX calculations, and report design for the cash flow statement.

By following these steps, you can create an interactive and informative cash flow statement in Power BI, empowering financial professionals and stakeholders to gain insights into a company's cash flows and financial performance.

Designing Balance Sheets

Balance sheets are fundamental financial reports that provide a snapshot of a company's financial position at a specific point in time. In this section, we'll guide you through the process of designing balance sheets in Power BI. We'll cover the necessary steps, data sources, calculations, and visualizations to build a comprehensive balance sheet report.

Steps to Design Balance Sheets in Power BI:

1. Data Sources:

   - Identify the data sources required to create a balance sheet. Common data sources include financial transaction records, general ledger data, and other financial data.

   Example: You may use tables containing asset, liability, and equity account balances.

2. Data Transformation:

   - Ensure that your financial data is cleaned, transformed, and properly structured. This may involve consolidating account balances, handling data formatting, and dealing with any missing values.

   Step-by-Step: Use Power Query in Power BI to perform data transformation and cleaning, as described in earlier sections.

3. Account Categories:

   - Group financial accounts into categories, such as assets, liabilities, and equity. Define measures for each category to organize your data.

   Example: Create measures that sum the total assets, total liabilities, and total equity.

4. Report Structure:

   - Design the structure of your balance sheet report. Create sections for assets, liabilities, and equity, and define the hierarchy of accounts within each category.

Step-by-Step: Use Power BI's report layout features to create sections, and arrange tables and visuals within each section.

5. Visualizations:

- Select visualizations to represent account balances within each category. Consider using tables, stacked bar charts, or treemaps to display the hierarchical structure.

Example: Use a stacked bar chart to show the composition of assets or liabilities by account.

6. Data Labels:

- Add labels to your visualizations to provide clarity and make it easier for users to interpret the data.

Step-by-Step: Include data labels and axis titles in your visualizations for account balances.

7. Interactive Features:

- Implement interactive features to enhance user experience. Users should be able to click on data points for additional details or switch between different reporting periods.

Example: Enable users to select different reporting dates and view historical balance sheets.

8. Data Validation:

- Validate the accuracy of your balance sheet by comparing it to external financial reports or other reliable sources. Ensure that the calculated balances align with accounting standards.

Step-by-Step: Compare the balance sheet results in Power BI with the balance sheet generated by your accounting system.

9. Data Trend Analysis:

   - Provide trend analysis by allowing users to compare balance sheets over multiple periods, such as months, quarters, or years.

   Example: Create a slicer that enables users to select different time periods for comparison.

10. Documentation:

   - Document the data sources, calculations, and report structure for future reference and auditing.

   Step-by-Step: Create documentation that explains the data sources, DAX calculations, and report design for the balance sheet.

By following these steps, you can create an interactive and informative balance sheet report in Power BI, empowering financial professionals and stakeholders to understand a company's financial position at a glance and make informed financial decisions.

Crafting Profit and Loss Statements

Profit and Loss (P&L) statements, also known as income statements, provide insights into a company's revenue, expenses, and profitability over a specific period. In this section, we'll guide you through the process of crafting Profit and Loss statements in Power BI. We'll cover the necessary steps, data sources, calculations, and visualizations to build a comprehensive P&L statement report.

Steps to Craft Profit and Loss Statements in Power BI:

1. Data Sources:

- Identify the data sources required to create a P&L statement. Common data sources include sales data, expense records, and financial transactions.

Example: You may use tables containing sales revenue, cost of goods sold, operating expenses, and other financial data.

2. Data Transformation:

- Ensure that your financial data is cleaned, transformed, and properly structured. This may involve aggregating revenue and expenses, handling data formatting, and addressing missing values.

Step-by-Step: Use Power Query in Power BI to perform data transformation and cleaning, as described in earlier sections.

3. Calculations:

- Calculate key financial metrics, including total revenue, gross profit, operating income, and net profit. These calculations are essential for a P&L statement.

Example: Calculate gross profit by subtracting the cost of goods sold from total revenue.

4. Revenue Categories:

- Group revenue into categories, such as product sales, service revenue, and other sources of income. Define measures for each revenue category.

Step-by-Step: Use DAX (Data Analysis Expressions) to create measures for different revenue categories.

5. Expense Categories:

- Group expenses into categories, such as cost of goods sold, operating expenses, and interest expenses. Define measures for each expense category.

Example: Create measures for total operating expenses and interest expenses.

6. Report Structure:

- Design the structure of your P&L statement report. Create sections for revenue, expenses, and profit metrics, and define the layout for each section.

Step-by-Step: Use Power BI's report layout features to create sections and arrange tables and visuals within each section.

7. Visualizations:

- Select visualizations to represent revenue, expenses, and profitability. Consider using tables, stacked column charts, or line charts for displaying trends.

Example: Use a stacked column chart to show the composition of revenue and expenses.

8. Data Labels:

- Add labels to your visualizations to provide clarity and make it easier for users to interpret the data.

Step-by-Step: Include data labels, axis titles, and data point tooltips in your visualizations.

9. Interactive Features:

- Implement interactive features to enhance user experience. Users should be able to click on data points for additional details or switch between different reporting periods.

Example: Enable users to select different reporting dates and view historical P&L statements.

10. Data Validation:

- Validate the accuracy of your P&L statement by comparing it to external financial reports or other reliable sources. Ensure that the calculated metrics align with accounting standards.

Step-by-Step: Compare the P&L statement results in Power BI with the statement generated by your accounting system.

11. Data Trend Analysis:

- Provide trend analysis by allowing users to compare P&L statements over multiple periods, such as months, quarters, or years.

Example: Create a slicer that enables users to select different time periods for comparison.

12. Documentation:

- Document the data sources, calculations, and report structure for future reference and auditing.

Step-by-Step: Create documentation that explains the data sources, DAX calculations, and report design for the P&L statement.

By following these steps, you can create an interactive and informative P&L statement in Power BI, empowering financial professionals and stakeholders to analyze a company's revenue, expenses, and profitability with ease.

2.3 Visualizing Financial Data

Introduction to Data Visualization

Data visualization is a critical aspect of financial reporting in Power BI. It involves representing financial data using charts, graphs, and visuals to make complex information more understandable and actionable. In this section, we'll introduce the fundamental concepts of data visualization and its significance in financial reporting.

Why Data Visualization Matters in Financial Reporting:

Data visualization serves several essential purposes in financial reporting:

1. Clarity and Comprehension: Complex financial data can be challenging to interpret. Visualization simplifies data, making it easier to understand for financial professionals and stakeholders.

2. Identification of Trends: Visualizations allow for the quick identification of trends, anomalies, and outliers within financial data, aiding in decision-making.

3. Comparison and Analysis: Visuals make it easy to compare different financial metrics and periods, enabling in-depth analysis.

4. Storytelling: Visualizations can tell a story, making it easier to convey financial insights and recommendations to non-experts.

Key Principles of Data Visualization:

When working with data visualization in Power BI for finance and accounting, consider these key principles:

1. Choose the Right Chart: Select the appropriate chart type for the data you want to visualize. Common chart types in financial reporting include bar charts, line charts, pie charts, and scatter plots.

   Example: Use a bar chart to display revenue by product category.

2. Simplify and Focus: Avoid clutter and complexity in your visuals. Keep your charts clean and focus on the most critical data points.

   Step-by-Step: Customize the visual appearance in Power BI to declutter and emphasize the key information.

3. Consistency: Maintain consistency in color schemes, labels, and formatting throughout your financial reports for better user experience.

   Step-by-Step: Create a template for your financial reports in Power BI to ensure consistency.

4. Interactivity: Use interactive features like slicers, filters, and drill-through capabilities to allow users to explore data and gain insights.

   Example: Implement a slicer for selecting different time periods in your reports.

5. Annotations and Labels: Include annotations, data labels, and tooltips to provide context and details on data points.

Step-by-Step: Add data labels and tooltips in Power BI visualizations.

6. Accessibility: Ensure that your visualizations are accessible to all users, including those with disabilities, by adhering to accessibility standards.

Step-by-Step: Use Power BI's accessibility features to make your reports inclusive.

Creating Your First Financial Reports with Data Visualization:

To start creating financial reports with data visualization in Power BI:

1. Import Data: Bring your financial data into Power BI, ensuring it is properly cleaned and structured.

2. Select Visualizations: Choose the most suitable visualizations for your data. For instance, use a line chart to visualize revenue trends over time.

3. Customize Visuals: Customize your visuals by adjusting colors, labels, and formatting to align with your organization's branding and standards.

4. Create Interactive Features: Implement interactive elements, such as slicers and filters, to allow users to explore the data.

5. Testing and Validation: Validate your reports for accuracy and user-friendliness, ensuring they align with accounting standards.

By following these principles and steps, you can effectively use data visualization to unlock financial insights in Power BI and create reports that provide valuable information to financial professionals and stakeholders.

Choosing the Right Charts for Financial Insights

Selecting the appropriate charts for visualizing financial data in Power BI is crucial for effective communication and analysis. In this section, we will explore various chart types commonly used in financial reporting and provide guidance on how to choose the right chart for different types of financial insights.

Common Chart Types for Financial Insights:

1. Bar Charts:

  - Best for: Comparing data across categories, such as comparing revenue by product or expenses by department.

  Example: Create a bar chart to compare the revenue generated by different product categories over a specific period.

2. Line Charts:

  - Best for: Displaying trends over time, like revenue growth or expense fluctuations.

  Example: Use a line chart to illustrate the revenue trend over the last twelve months.

3. Pie Charts:

  - Best for: Showing the composition of a whole in percentage, like the distribution of expenses in various categories.

Example: Create a pie chart to represent the proportion of operating expenses in the overall budget.

4. Scatter Plots:

- Best for: Analyzing the relationship between two variables, like the correlation between marketing expenses and sales.

Example: Utilize a scatter plot to examine the relationship between advertising spending and revenue.

5. Stacked Bar Charts:

- Best for: Comparing data across categories while also showing the composition of each category.

Example: Build a stacked bar chart to compare the total expenses by department and display the composition of expenses within each department.

6. Treemaps:

- Best for: Visualizing hierarchical data structures, such as showing the breakdown of expenses from high-level categories to detailed subcategories.

Example: Use a treemap to display the expense hierarchy from broad categories (e.g., "Operational Expenses") down to subcategories (e.g., "Office Supplies").

Selecting the Right Chart:

When choosing the right chart for your financial insights, consider the following steps:

1. Understand Your Data: Grasp the nature of your financial data, whether it's categorical, numerical, or temporal. This understanding will guide your choice of chart type.

2. Determine Your Message: Clarify the key message you want to convey with the chart. Are you comparing, showing trends, or illustrating proportions?

3. Consider the Audience: Think about who will be using the report and their familiarity with different chart types. Ensure that the chart is accessible and understandable to your target audience.

4. Visual Appeal: Ensure that the chart is visually appealing and easy to interpret. Pay attention to color choices, labels, and formatting.

5. Use Interactive Features: Implement interactivity, such as tooltips and drill-through options, to allow users to explore the data further.

6. Validate Accuracy: Verify that the chart accurately represents the underlying financial data.

Example Use Case:

Suppose you want to compare the revenue generated by different product categories in your company over the last quarter. In this case, a horizontal bar chart can effectively display this information, with each product category represented by a bar, and the length of the bar indicating the revenue.

Step-by-Step Guide:

1. Import your financial data into Power BI, ensuring it includes product categories and corresponding revenue figures.

2. Create a horizontal bar chart in Power BI, with product categories on the y-axis and revenue on the x-axis.

3. Customize the chart's appearance with colors and labels to enhance clarity.

4. Enable tooltips to provide additional details when users hover over the bars.

By following these steps and considering the nature of your data and the message you want to convey, you can select the right chart type for your financial insights effectively.

Creating Your First Financial Reports

In this section, we will walk you through the process of creating your first financial reports in Power BI. Financial reports are essential for monitoring and communicating financial performance within an organization. Power BI enables you to design interactive and visually appealing financial reports that provide insights at a glance.

Step 1: Data Import and Transformation

Before you can create financial reports, you need to import and transform your financial data. Follow these steps:

1. Data Import: Import your financial data into Power BI. This data can include information such as revenue, expenses, profit, and various financial metrics.

2. Data Transformation: Clean and transform your data as needed. This may involve handling missing values, formatting dates, and creating calculated columns.

Step 2: Data Modeling

To create effective financial reports, you'll want to establish a data model that defines relationships between different data tables. Common relationships include connecting a sales table to a products table or a time table.

Step 3: Report Layout

Now, let's start building your financial reports:

1. Creating Visuals: Select the type of visuals (charts, tables, matrices, etc.) that best represent your financial data. For instance, you can use a line chart to display revenue trends over time.

2. Data Visualization: Add data fields to your visuals. For example, in a bar chart, you might add the "Product Category" to the axis and "Revenue" to the values.

3. Page Layout: Organize your visuals on report pages. You can create multiple pages to focus on different aspects of financial data.

Step 4: Interaction and Exploration

One of the key advantages of Power BI is its interactivity. Enable features like drill-through, slicers, and cross-filtering to allow users to interact with and explore the data.

Step 5: Formatting and Design

Ensure that your financial reports are visually appealing and easy to understand:

1. Color and Theme: Apply a consistent color scheme and theme to your report.

2. Labels and Titles: Use clear and informative labels and titles for visuals and pages.

Step 6: Publish and Share

Once you've created your financial reports, publish them to the Power BI service or share them with your team. This enables others to access the reports and explore the financial data.

Example Use Case:

Suppose you want to create a financial report that displays the revenue and expenses of your company over the last fiscal year. You can import your financial data, create visuals like line charts for revenue and expenses, establish a page layout, add interaction features, and then publish the report to share with your team.

By following these steps, you can design compelling financial reports that provide valuable insights and aid in informed decision-making within your organization.

CHAPTER III
Advanced Financial Reporting with Power BI

3.1 Interactive Financial Dashboards

Designing Interactive Financial Dashboards

Interactive financial dashboards are a powerful tool in Power BI for finance and accounting professionals. They allow users to explore financial data, gain insights, and make data-driven decisions. In this section, we will guide you through the process of designing interactive financial dashboards.

Step 1: Define Your Dashboard's Purpose

Before you begin designing your financial dashboard, it's essential to have a clear understanding of its purpose. Are you creating a dashboard to track sales performance, monitor expenses, or analyze profitability? Define your key objectives.

Step 2: Data Preparation

To create an interactive dashboard, you need well-organized and clean financial data. Here's what you should do:

1. Data Import: Import your financial data into Power BI, including datasets for revenue, expenses, and any other relevant metrics.

2. Data Transformation: Clean and prepare your data. Address missing values, format dates, and create calculated columns as needed.

Step 3: Select Visualizations

Choose the right visualizations to represent your financial data. Power BI offers a wide range of visuals, such as charts, tables, and matrices. For financial dashboards, common visuals include:

- Line Charts: To show trends over time, like revenue and expenses.

- Pie Charts: For displaying the composition of expenses or revenue by category.

- Tables and Matrices: To present detailed financial data.

Step 4: Building the Dashboard

Now, let's create your interactive financial dashboard:

1. Canvas Layout: Arrange visuals on the canvas. Consider the layout, the number of pages, and how users will navigate through the dashboard.

2. Filters and Slicers: Implement filters and slicers for interactivity. For instance, you can add slicers for date ranges, product categories, or departments.

3. Drill-Through: Enable drill-through actions to allow users to explore data at a more granular level. For example, clicking on a chart could provide more detailed information.

Step 5: Dynamic Financial Reporting

To make your financial dashboard dynamic, you can use features like bookmarks and buttons. Here's how:

1. Bookmarks: Create bookmarks for different views of your dashboard. For example, you can set up bookmarks for monthly, quarterly, and yearly financial views.

2. Buttons: Add buttons for navigation between bookmarks. Users can switch between different views with a single click.

Step 6: User Testing and Refinement

After designing your interactive financial dashboard, it's crucial to gather feedback from potential users and make any necessary refinements. Ensure that the dashboard meets the needs of its users and provides valuable insights.

Example Use Case:

Suppose you are designing an interactive financial dashboard to track monthly sales and expenses. You import your financial data, create line charts for revenue and expenses, add slicers for selecting date ranges, and implement bookmarks for monthly, quarterly, and yearly views. Users can click on the buttons to switch between different time frames.

By following these steps, you can create an interactive financial dashboard that empowers users to explore financial data, gain insights, and make informed decisions.

I hope this section helps you understand how to design interactive financial dashboards in Power BI effectively. If you have any specific questions or need further details, feel free to ask.

Implementing Slicers and Filters

Slicers and filters are essential components of interactive financial dashboards in Power BI. They allow users to dynamically control and customize the data they want to see. In this section, we will explore how to effectively implement slicers and filters in your financial reports.

Step 1: Choose Data Fields for Slicers and Filters

Before implementing slicers and filters, you need to decide which data fields users will interact with. For financial reports, common choices include:

- Date Slicers: Allow users to select date ranges for data analysis.

- Category Filters: Enable users to filter data by product categories, departments, or any other relevant categories.

- Value Slicers: Provide options to filter by specific financial values, such as revenue thresholds.

Step 2: Adding Slicers and Filters to Your Dashboard

Here's how to add slicers and filters to your Power BI financial dashboard:

1. Insert Slicers: In Power BI Desktop, go to the "Visualizations" pane, select "Slicer," and drag the desired data field into the slicer area.

2. Customize Slicers: Customize slicers' appearance, such as layout, font, and style. You can also choose between single-select or multi-select options, depending on your users' needs.

Step 3: Filter Interaction Options

Now, you can determine how slicers and filters interact with other visuals on your dashboard:

1. Filtering Charts: Link slicers to other visuals on your dashboard. When users select a specific date range or category, related charts and tables will automatically adjust to display filtered data.

2. Visual-Level Filters: Implement visual-level filters, which allow individual visuals to have their own filters. This can provide more flexibility in your dashboard's design.

Step 4: Dynamic Financial Reporting

Slicers and filters make your financial reports dynamic and responsive to user inputs. Here's how to enhance the interactivity:

1. Clear Filters: Add a "Clear Filters" button or option to reset all slicers and filters, returning the dashboard to its initial state.

2. Dynamic Titles: Create dynamic titles that reflect the selected slicer or filter criteria. This provides context and clarity to users.

Example Use Case:

Let's say you're designing a financial dashboard for analyzing sales data. You add date slicers to allow users to choose a date range, and category filters to filter data by product categories. When a user selects a specific date range and category, all charts and tables in the dashboard automatically update to display relevant sales information.

By implementing slicers and filters effectively, users can tailor their financial analysis to their specific needs and gain valuable insights.

Dynamic Financial Reporting

Dynamic financial reporting in Power BI goes beyond static reports and enables users to explore and analyze financial data interactively. With dynamic reporting, users can gain insights tailored to their needs and make informed decisions. In this section, we'll delve into creating dynamic financial reports in Power BI.

Step 1: Building Interactive Visuals

To create dynamic financial reports, start by designing interactive visuals that respond to user actions. Here's how:

1. Create Visuals: Use Power BI's visualizations to build charts, tables, and visuals that represent financial data. Choose visuals that best convey your financial information.

2. Link Visuals: Ensure that the visuals are linked to each other. When one visual is selected or filtered, other related visuals should adjust accordingly.

Step 2: Utilizing Slicers and Filters

Slicers and filters play a crucial role in making your financial reports dynamic. They allow users to control what they see. To implement dynamic reporting:

1. Add Slicers: Include slicers for parameters like date ranges, product categories, or financial metrics. Users can interact with these slicers to refine the data they view.

2. Interactions: Configure interactions between slicers and visuals. Define how visuals respond when slicers are used. For instance, selecting a date range should filter data in all visuals on the report.

Step 3: Creating Dynamic Measures

Dynamic financial reporting may involve measures that adapt to user selections. For example, you may want to display a rolling total for the selected date range. To create dynamic measures:

1. DAX Formulas: Use DAX (Data Analysis Expressions) to write custom formulas that respond to slicer selections. For instance, create a DAX formula for calculating rolling totals based on selected dates.

2. Measure Tables: Organize these dynamic measures in separate measure tables to maintain clarity and organization.

Step 4: Implementing Drill-Through

Drill-through functionality allows users to explore more detailed information. Here's how to set up drill-through:

1. Create Drill-Through Pages: Design additional report pages that provide detailed information on specific aspects of financial data.

2. Define Drill-Through Fields: Specify which fields in your data model can be used for drill-through actions. For example, you might enable drill-through on product names to access detailed product data.

3. Interactive Buttons: Add interactive buttons or visuals that trigger drill-through actions when clicked.

Example Use Case:

Imagine you're developing a dynamic financial report for sales analysis. Users can select a date range and product category from slicers. The report's visuals automatically update to show sales trends and product performance for the chosen parameters. You've also incorporated drill-through functionality, allowing users to click on a product to see a detailed breakdown of sales by region and customer.

Dynamic financial reporting empowers users to explore data, discover insights, and make data-driven decisions tailored to their specific needs.

3.2 Data Modeling in Power BI

Understanding Data Modeling Concepts

Data modeling is a fundamental aspect of Power BI that underpins the creation of effective financial reports. To harness the full power of Power BI for finance and accounting, it's essential to grasp the core concepts of data modeling.

What is Data Modeling?

Data modeling involves structuring your data to represent real-world entities, their attributes, and the relationships between them. In Power BI, data modeling is mainly about defining your data model using tables, relationships, and calculated measures.

Key Concepts:

1. Tables: In Power BI, a table is a collection of data. Each table represents a specific entity, such as customers, products, or financial transactions. For example, you might have a 'Sales' table containing sales data.

2. Columns: Tables consist of columns that define the attributes of the entity. Each column contains specific types of data, such as numbers, text, or dates. For instance, a 'Customers' table might have columns like 'CustomerName' and 'CustomerID.'

3. Relationships: Relationships establish connections between tables. For example, a 'Sales' table may have a relationship with a 'Customers' table via the 'CustomerID' column. This enables you to associate each sale with a specific customer.

4. Calculated Measures: Calculated measures are custom calculations created using DAX (Data Analysis Expressions). They provide insights and aggregations not present in the raw data. For instance, you can calculate total sales, average revenue, or year-to-date growth.

Steps to Understand Data Modeling:

1. Identify Entities: Begin by identifying the entities or objects you want to analyze in your financial reports. These might include sales, expenses, assets, liabilities, and equity.

2. Define Tables: Create tables for each entity. Populate these tables with relevant columns. For a 'Sales' table, you might have columns like 'Date,' 'Product,' 'Quantity,' and 'Revenue.'

3. Establish Relationships: Determine how these tables are related. A common practice is to use unique identifiers, such as customer IDs or product IDs, to link tables. You can specify relationships in Power BI's relationship view.

4. Create Calculated Measures: Use DAX to build calculated measures that provide valuable financial insights. For instance, you can create measures for net profit margin, return on investment (ROI), or current ratio.

Example:

Let's consider a financial modeling example. You're working with sales data and have tables for 'Sales,' 'Customers,' and 'Products.' By establishing relationships between these tables, you can create calculated measures that show metrics like 'Total Sales,' 'Average Revenue per Customer,' and 'Sales by Product Category.'

Data modeling forms the foundation for meaningful financial analysis in Power BI. A well-structured data model enables you to create informative visuals and reports that drive financial decision-making.

Building Data Models for Finance

Building effective data models is a crucial step in harnessing the full potential of Power BI for financial reporting. A well-structured data model allows you to analyze financial data with precision and generate meaningful insights. In this section, we will explore the process of building data models tailored to finance.

Steps to Build Data Models for Finance:

1. Data Source Selection: The first step is to identify the data sources for your financial analysis. Common sources include accounting software, databases, spreadsheets, and online services. Choose sources that provide the relevant financial data.

2. Data Extraction: Extract the required financial data from your chosen sources. This often involves exporting data in formats like Excel, CSV, or connecting directly to databases. Ensure data integrity during the extraction process.

3. Data Transformation: Financial data may require cleaning and transformation to make it suitable for analysis. Common tasks include handling missing values, standardizing date formats, and converting currencies if dealing with international data.

4. Table Creation: In Power BI, create tables to represent key financial entities, such as 'Income Statements,' 'Balance Sheets,' and 'Cash Flow Statements.' Each table should contain relevant columns representing line items and financial metrics.

5. Defining Relationships: Establish relationships between tables based on common keys like date, account, or product ID. These relationships allow you to combine data from different tables for comprehensive analysis.

6. Creating Calculated Columns: Calculate columns in your tables that are not directly present in the raw data. For example, you can calculate net profit by subtracting expenses from revenue.

7. Measures with DAX: Utilize Data Analysis Expressions (DAX) to create custom financial measures. DAX functions enable you to calculate metrics like net profit margin, return on investment (ROI), or financial ratios.

Example: Building a Data Model for Financial Statements

Let's say you're building a data model for financial statements. You have extracted data from your accounting software and created tables for 'Income Statements' and 'Balance Sheets.' These tables include columns for dates, accounts, and values. By establishing relationships and crafting calculated columns, you can generate key financial metrics like net income, total assets, and liabilities.

Power BI's intuitive interface makes it easy to create relationships, define calculations, and measure financial performance.

Best Practices:

- Ensure data quality and accuracy.

- Maintain a clear and consistent naming convention for tables and columns.

- Use a date table to facilitate time-based analysis.

- Regularly update your data model to reflect new financial data.

By following these steps and best practices, you'll have a robust data model ready for in-depth financial analysis and reporting.

Calculations and Measures in DAX

Data Analysis Expressions (DAX) is a powerful formula language used in Power BI to create custom calculations and measures. In the context of finance and accounting, DAX allows you to calculate specific financial metrics, ratios, and other analytical insights. In this section, we will delve into the world of DAX for financial reporting.

Understanding DAX:

DAX is designed to work with tables of data and perform calculations across those tables. It is similar to Excel functions, but more powerful and suited for handling large datasets. DAX is commonly used for creating calculated columns and measures.

Steps to Create Calculations and Measures in DAX:

1. Understanding Calculated Columns vs. Measures:

   - *Calculated Columns*: These are columns added to your data model that contain calculated values based on expressions or formulas. Calculated columns become part of the underlying table and are precomputed.

   - *Measures*: Measures are dynamic calculations that provide results on the fly. They are especially useful for aggregations and calculations that vary based on user interactions.

2. Creating Calculated Columns:

   - To create a calculated column, go to the Data View in Power BI Desktop.

- Right-click on a table and select "New Column."

- Write a DAX formula to define the calculated column's behavior. For example, to calculate the gross profit, you can use the formula: `[Gross Profit] = [Revenue] - [Cost]`.

3. Creating Measures:

   - To create a measure, go to the Data View in Power BI Desktop.

   - In the modeling tab, click "New Measure."

   - Write a DAX expression to calculate the desired financial metric. For instance, you can create a measure for profit margin using the formula: `Profit Margin = DIVIDE([Gross Profit], [Revenue])`.

Example: Calculating Key Financial Metrics

Let's say you want to calculate important financial metrics, such as profit margin, return on investment (ROI), or liquidity ratios. You can use DAX measures to perform these calculations based on the data in your financial tables. DAX is versatile and can handle complex financial logic with ease.

Best Practices:

- Optimize your DAX formulas for performance.

- Keep DAX calculations simple and efficient.

- Document your DAX measures for clarity and future reference.

- Test and validate your DAX calculations to ensure accuracy.

By mastering DAX, you can unlock the full potential of Power BI for financial reporting, enabling you to generate meaningful insights from your financial data.

I hope this section provides you with a comprehensive understanding of how to perform calculations and create measures using DAX in the context of financial reporting with Power BI.

3.3 Advanced Financial Metrics

Calculating Key Financial Ratios

Calculating key financial ratios is crucial for financial analysis and decision-making. In Power BI, you can leverage DAX (Data Analysis Expressions) to create measures that calculate these ratios. Let's explore how to calculate some of the most important financial ratios using DAX.

1. Liquidity Ratios:

- Current Ratio measures a company's ability to cover its short-term liabilities with short-term assets. The formula is: `Current Ratio = [Current Assets] / [Current Liabilities]`.

- Quick Ratio (Acid-Test Ratio) evaluates a company's short-term liquidity, excluding inventory from current assets. The formula is: `Quick Ratio = ([Current Assets] - [Inventory]) / [Current Liabilities]`.

2. Profitability Ratios:

- Net Profit Margin shows the percentage of revenue that remains as profit after all expenses. The formula is: `Net Profit Margin = DIVIDE([Net Profit], [Revenue])`.

- Gross Profit Margin indicates the percentage of revenue retained as gross profit. The formula is: `Gross Profit Margin = DIVIDE([Gross Profit], [Revenue])`.

3. Efficiency Ratios:

- Accounts Receivable Turnover measures how quickly a company collects payments from its customers. The formula is: `Accounts Receivable Turnover = DIVIDE([Revenue], [Average Accounts Receivable])`.

- Inventory Turnover assesses how effectively a company manages its inventory. The formula is: `Inventory Turnover = DIVIDE([Cost of Goods Sold], [Average Inventory])`.

4. Leverage Ratios:

- Debt to Equity Ratio evaluates the proportion of debt used to finance the company relative to shareholders' equity. The formula is: `Debt to Equity Ratio = DIVIDE([Total Debt], [Shareholders' Equity])`.

Steps to Create DAX Measures for Ratios:

1. Open your Power BI report and go to the Data View.

2. Click on the "New Measure" button.

3. Write a DAX formula that corresponds to the ratio you want to calculate. For example, to calculate the Current Ratio, use the formula: `Current Ratio = DIVIDE([Current Assets], [Current Liabilities])`.

4. Test your measure by adding it to your visuals. Ensure it provides the correct ratio value.

Best Practices:

- Use meaningful names for your measures to enhance clarity.

- Document your DAX measures for reference and sharing.

- Ensure your data model is structured correctly with the necessary tables and relationships.

By creating DAX measures for key financial ratios, you can gain valuable insights into a company's financial health, which is essential for informed decision-making and strategic planning.

Forecasting and Scenario Analysis

Forecasting and scenario analysis are essential for financial planning and decision-making. Power BI allows you to create forecasts and explore different scenarios using your financial data. Let's walk through the process of forecasting and conducting scenario analysis in Power BI.

Creating a Forecast:

1. Data Preparation: Ensure your financial data is clean, complete, and well-structured.

2. Time-Series Data: Financial forecasting often involves time-series data, such as monthly revenue figures. Make sure you have a date or time column in your data.

3. Creating a Visual: In Power BI, select the visual where you want to display the forecast, such as a line chart or area chart.

4. Access Forecasting Options:

   - Click on the visual.

   - In the "Visualizations" pane, go to "Analytics."

- Choose "Forecast."

5. Configure Forecast Options:

  - Set the forecasting period (e.g., the number of periods to forecast).

  - Specify the confidence interval (e.g., 95%).

  - Adjust other options like seasonality and prediction intervals as needed.

6. Generate the Forecast: Power BI will generate a forecast line on your chart based on historical data.

Scenario Analysis:

Scenario analysis involves exploring different what-if scenarios based on your financial data. You can use Power BI to create multiple scenarios and assess their impact.

Steps for Scenario Analysis:

1. Create a Base Scenario: Duplicate your existing data or visual and make it the base scenario. For instance, if you want to analyze the impact of price changes, create a duplicate of your revenue data.

2. Modify Data for Scenarios: Adjust the duplicated data to reflect the changes you want to analyze. For example, change product prices in the duplicated dataset.

3. Combine Scenarios: You can create multiple duplicated visuals or tables for different scenarios, each with its changes.

4. Use Filters and Slicers: Set up filters and slicers in your report to easily switch between scenarios. You can create slicers for different scenarios and allow users to select which scenario they want to view.

5. Visualize the Impact: Create visuals to compare the base scenario with different scenarios side by side. This could include charts, tables, or KPI cards.

Best Practices:

- Ensure your data model is well-organized to support both forecasting and scenario analysis.

- Use clear and meaningful names for visuals and scenarios.

- Document your scenarios and assumptions for reference.

By forecasting and conducting scenario analysis in Power BI, you can gain insights into potential future outcomes and make data-driven decisions for your organization.

Detecting Anomalies and Trends

Detecting anomalies and trends in financial data is crucial for identifying potential issues and opportunities. Power BI offers various tools and techniques to help you uncover anomalies and trends effectively. Let's explore how to do this.

Anomaly Detection:

1. Data Preparation: Start by ensuring your financial data is clean, complete, and structured. Anomalies can often arise from data quality issues.

2. Choose a Visual: Select a visual representation of your financial data, such as a line chart or scatter plot.

3. Visualize Data Trends: Visualize your data to identify any obvious trends or patterns.

4. Use Analytics in Power BI:

   - Click on your visual.

   - In the "Visualizations" pane, go to "Analytics."

   - Select "Anomalies."

5. Configure Anomaly Detection:

   - Choose the column that you want to analyze for anomalies.

   - Specify parameters like sensitivity and severity.

6. View Anomalies: Power BI will highlight data points that deviate significantly from the expected pattern, helping you identify anomalies.

Trend Analysis:

1. Data Preparation: Ensure your data includes a date or time column, as trends are often time-dependent.

2. Choose the Right Visual: Select a visual that best represents your data. Line charts, area charts, and bar charts are often used for trend analysis.

3. Create Visuals: Build visuals that show the data over time or other relevant dimensions.

4. Use Analytics in Power BI:

  - Click on your visual.

  - In the "Visualizations" pane, go to "Analytics."

  - Select "Trend Line."

5. Configure Trend Analysis:

  - Specify the column to analyze for trends.

  - Adjust options like confidence intervals and forecasting periods.

6. View Trends: Power BI will add trend lines to your visual, helping you visualize and understand trends in your data.

Best Practices:

- Choose the right visualizations to effectively highlight anomalies and trends.

- Document any detected anomalies, and investigate their potential causes.

- Regularly update your data to ensure that your anomaly detection and trend analysis remain relevant.

By leveraging Power BI's capabilities for anomaly detection and trend analysis, you can gain deeper insights into your financial data and make more informed decisions.

CHAPTER IV
Deploying Financial Reports with Power BI

4.1 Sharing and Collaboration

Sharing Financial Reports

Sharing financial reports with stakeholders is a critical step in the reporting process. Power BI offers several options for sharing your reports with various audiences. Let's explore how to effectively share financial reports.

Option 1: Publish to the Power BI Service:

1. Publish Your Report:

   - In Power BI Desktop, click on "Publish."

   - Select the workspace where you want to publish the report.

   - Click "Publish."

2. Share with Stakeholders:

   - Go to the Power BI Service (https://app.powerbi.com).

   - Open your report.

3. Share the Report:

  - Click on the "File" menu in the Power BI Service.

  - Select "Publish to web" to create a public link, or choose "Share."

  - Enter the email addresses of your stakeholders.

  - Customize permissions (e.g., view, edit) as needed.

  - Share the report with stakeholders.

Option 2: Embed in SharePoint or Other Platforms:

1. Publish Your Report:

  - In Power BI Desktop, click on "Publish."

  - Select the workspace.

2. Share the Embedded Code:

  - In the Power BI Service, locate your report.

  - Click on "File" and select "Embed report."

  - Generate an embed code.

3. Integrate with SharePoint:

  - In SharePoint or other platforms, create a page or section where you want to embed the report.

  - Insert the generated embed code.

  - Share the page with stakeholders.

Option 3: Export Reports as PDF or PowerPoint:

1. Design Your Report:

   - In Power BI Desktop, format your report for exporting.

   - Arrange visuals and pages as needed.

2. Export as PDF or PowerPoint:

   - In Power BI Desktop, click on "File."

   - Select "Export," then choose "PDF" or "PowerPoint."

   - Customize settings such as page size, layout, and quality.

   - Save the exported file.

3. Distribute the Exported File:

   - Share the exported PDF or PowerPoint file via email, file-sharing services, or your organization's preferred communication channels.

Best Practices:

- Clearly define the roles and permissions for your stakeholders (e.g., view-only, edit) when sharing within the Power BI Service.

- Ensure that you have proper data security measures in place to protect sensitive financial data.

- Periodically update and refresh your shared reports to keep stakeholders informed with the latest data.

By following these steps and best practices, you can efficiently share financial reports with stakeholders using Power BI.

Collaborative Workspaces in Power BI

Collaborative workspaces in Power BI play a crucial role in enabling teams to work together effectively, share reports, and collaborate on data analysis. These workspaces provide a centralized location for teams to access and collaborate on financial reports. Here's how to set up and use collaborative workspaces in Power BI:

Creating a Collaborative Workspace:

1. Log in to Power BI Service:

   - Access the Power BI Service at https://app.powerbi.com.

2. Create a Workspace:

   - Click on "Workspaces" on the left-hand navigation pane.

   - Select "Create a workspace."

3. Name and Describe the Workspace:

   - Give your workspace a name and description.

   - Choose the visibility (e.g., "My workspace" for personal use or "Shared workspace" for collaboration).

4. Add Members:

   - Under the "Access" tab, add members to your workspace by entering their email addresses.

   - Specify their roles (e.g., Member or Admin) and access permissions.

Uploading Reports to a Workspace:

1. Open the Workspace:

   - Click on the workspace you've created.

2. Upload Reports:

   - Navigate to the "Reports" tab.

   - Click "Publish app" and select the reports you want to upload.

3. Configure Report Settings:

   - Customize the settings for your uploaded reports, such as visuals, filters, and navigation.

Collaborating in a Workspace:

1. Collaborate with Team Members:

   - Members of the workspace can access and collaborate on the reports.

   - They can make comments, ask questions, and provide insights directly within the reports.

2. Data Source Integration:

   - Ensure that your data sources are connected and updated regularly to provide the latest financial data to your team.

Sharing Reports from a Workspace:

1. Share Reports:

   - From the workspace, select the report you want to share.

- Click on "File" and choose "Publish to web" or "Share."

2. Manage Permissions:

  - Define the sharing settings and access permissions for the report within the workspace.

Best Practices:

- Regularly update and refresh the data in your reports to keep the information current.

- Clearly communicate roles and responsibilities within the collaborative workspace.

- Train team members on how to effectively use Power BI's collaboration features.

By setting up and utilizing collaborative workspaces in Power BI, you can enhance teamwork and streamline financial reporting within your organization.

Exporting and Printing Reports

Exporting and printing reports in Power BI is essential for sharing insights with stakeholders who may prefer physical copies or different file formats. Power BI offers various options for exporting and printing reports, making it flexible and convenient. Here's how to export and print your financial reports:

Exporting Reports:

1. Open the Report:

  - In Power BI Service, navigate to the report you want to export.

2. Access the Export Option:

  - Click on the "File" menu in the report.

3. Choose the Export Format:

  - Select "Export" and then pick the format you want (e.g., PDF, PPT, Excel).

4. Set Export Options:

  - Configure export options such as page size, orientation, and the current page or all pages.

  - If you select "PDF" format, you can choose between portrait and landscape mode and customize margins.

5. Export the Report:

  - Click the "Export" button to generate the report in the chosen format.

6. Download or Share:

  - Depending on your browser settings, the file will either download to your computer or open for viewing.

Printing Reports:

1. Open the Report:

  - Access the report you wish to print.

2. Access the Print Option:

  - Click on the "File" menu and choose "Print."

3. Customize Printing Settings:

   - Configure printing settings such as page layout, size, and margins.

4. Print the Report:

   - Click the "Print" button to send the report to your printer.

Best Practices:

- When exporting reports to different formats, ensure that the layout and formatting are suitable for the chosen format.

- Test printing settings to achieve the desired output on paper.

- Make sure that page sizes and orientations match the report design for a professional look.

By mastering the export and printing options in Power BI, you can efficiently share your financial reports with stakeholders in their preferred formats, whether digital or hardcopy.

4.2 Automated Data Updates

Scheduling Data Refresh

In Power BI, scheduling data refresh is essential to ensure that your reports and dashboards are always up-to-date with the latest data from your sources. By scheduling automatic data refresh, you can avoid the manual process of data updates. Here's how to schedule data refresh:

Setting up Scheduled Data Refresh:

1. Publish Your Report:

   - Ensure that your Power BI report is published to the Power BI service. You need a Power BI Pro or Premium license to enable scheduled data refresh.

2. Access the Dataset Settings:

   - In the Power BI service, navigate to the dataset that your report is based on.

3. Configure Data Source Credentials:

   - Under "Settings" or "More options" for the dataset, set up data source credentials. You may need to provide login credentials or connection information for your data sources. This is crucial for accessing the data.

4. Schedule Data Refresh:

   - Find the "Scheduled refresh" section in the dataset settings. You can specify the frequency and time zone for data refresh.

5. Configure Refresh Options:

- Customize the refresh options, such as enabling background data refresh and setting up a retry schedule in case of any issues.

6. Save Settings:

- Save the refresh settings, and Power BI will automatically refresh your data according to the schedule you defined.

Monitoring Refresh Status:

1. Check Refresh History:

- You can view the refresh history to monitor the status of each refresh operation. If there are any errors, you'll find detailed information to diagnose the issue.

2. Set Up Notifications:

- Configure email notifications to be informed of any refresh failures or other issues.

Best Practices:

- Ensure that your data sources are configured to allow access for scheduled refresh. If they require authentication, keep the credentials up to date.

- Regularly review and test your scheduled refresh settings, especially when changes are made to the data sources or data model.

By scheduling data refresh in Power BI, you can automate the process of updating your reports, saving time and ensuring your financial data is always current for decision-making.

Integrating Data from Multiple Sources

One of the powerful features of Power BI is its ability to integrate data from multiple sources, allowing you to create comprehensive financial reports. Here's a step-by-step guide on how to integrate data from various sources:

1. Open Power BI Desktop:

   - Launch Power BI Desktop, which is the tool for creating and transforming data before publishing it to the Power BI service.

2. Click on 'Home' and Select 'Get Data':

   - In Power BI Desktop, go to the 'Home' tab, and click on 'Get Data.' This action will open a dialog box with various data source options.

3. Choose Data Sources:

   - Power BI supports a wide range of data sources, including databases (SQL Server, Oracle, MySQL), files (Excel, CSV), online services (Azure, SharePoint), and many others. Select the relevant data sources you want to integrate.

4. Configure Data Source Connections:

   - For each data source you select, you will need to configure the connection. This may involve specifying server details, authentication credentials, and database or file locations.

5. Load Data:

   - After configuring the data sources, click 'Load' to import the data into Power BI Desktop. It's possible to load data from multiple sources in the same report.

6. Data Transformation:

- Use Power Query, an integrated tool in Power BI, to transform and clean the data. You can filter rows, merge tables, create calculated columns, and perform various data transformation tasks.

7. Create Relationships:

- If your data comes from different sources and you want to analyze it together, establish relationships between tables. Power BI will help you identify and create relationships based on common fields.

8. Data Model Creation:

- Once your data is loaded and relationships are defined, create a data model. This model serves as the foundation for your financial reports and visualizations.

9. Data Modeling and Calculations:

- Use Data Analysis Expressions (DAX) to create calculations and measures that provide insights into your financial data. DAX allows you to perform calculations like totals, averages, and growth rates.

10. Visualization:

- Build reports and dashboards using the integrated Power BI visualization tools. You can create visualizations such as charts, tables, and graphs to represent your financial data.

11. Publish to Power BI Service:

- After creating your report in Power BI Desktop, publish it to the Power BI service, where it can be accessed and shared with stakeholders.

By integrating data from multiple sources, you can create comprehensive financial reports that provide a holistic view of your financial data.

Managing Data Security

Effective data security is paramount when dealing with financial data. Power BI provides various features and methods to manage data security, ensuring that only authorized individuals can access sensitive financial information. Here's a step-by-step guide on how to manage data security in Power BI:

1. Power BI Service:

   - To manage data security, you'll need to utilize the Power BI service, which allows you to create, share, and publish reports securely.

2. Data Sources Access Control:

   - In Power BI, you can control data source access by configuring permissions for data sources, like databases and files. Ensure that only authorized users have access to these sources.

3. Dataset-Level Security:

   - Power BI provides the ability to implement dataset-level security. This allows you to restrict access to specific datasets based on user roles and filters. To set up dataset-level security:

   - a. Define Roles: Create roles in Power BI, such as 'Finance Manager' and 'Sales Team,' based on your organization's requirements.

   - b. Define Row-Level Security Filters: Create filters that restrict access to specific data rows for each role. For instance, you can limit access to financial data for a specific region or department.

   - c. Assign Roles to Users: Assign users or groups to the appropriate roles in Power BI.

4. Row-Level Security:

- Row-level security is a critical feature for financial reporting. It allows you to filter data at the row level based on user context. For example, a sales manager will only see sales data for their region. Implement row-level security by defining rules and assigning them to specific roles.

5. Service Access Controls:

- In the Power BI service, you can control who has access to your published reports and dashboards. You can choose to share content with specific users, groups, or the entire organization.

6. Embed Codes and APIs:

- If you embed Power BI reports in your applications, ensure that you use authentication and authorization mechanisms to control access to the embedded reports.

7. Audit Logs and Monitoring:

- Regularly monitor the usage of your reports and dashboards. Power BI provides audit logs that can help you track who accesses your financial reports.

8. Compliance and Encryption:

- Ensure that your data complies with industry standards and regulations. Power BI provides encryption and compliance features to protect your data.

9. Data Loss Prevention (DLP):

- Use Power BI's Data Loss Prevention policies to prevent sensitive data from being shared inappropriately.

10. User Training:

   - Ensure that users accessing financial data are aware of security best practices and adhere to the policies in place.

Implementing robust data security measures is crucial to protecting sensitive financial information and ensuring compliance with privacy and security standards.

4.3 Real-world Use Cases

Case Studies: How Organizations Benefit from Power BI

Power BI has proven to be a powerful tool for organizations in the finance and accounting sector. Here, we'll explore real-world case studies that illustrate how various companies have leveraged Power BI to unlock financial insights, streamline their processes, and make data-driven decisions.

Case Study 1: Financial Performance Dashboard

Background:

  - A multinational corporation operating in various sectors needed to monitor its financial performance across multiple regions and business units.

Solution:

  - The company implemented Power BI to create a comprehensive financial performance dashboard. The dashboard integrated data from various sources, providing real-time insights into revenue, expenses, and profit margins.

Benefits:

  - With the Power BI dashboard, the organization could:

    - Monitor financial KPIs in real-time.

    - Identify underperforming business units and take corrective actions.

    - Improve decision-making by visualizing data.

Case Study 2: Budget Management and Forecasting

Background:

- A medium-sized enterprise in the retail industry faced challenges in managing its budgets and forecasting sales.

Solution:

- The company integrated Power BI with its financial systems to create budget management and forecasting reports. These reports allowed them to set realistic financial targets and track their progress.

Benefits:

- With Power BI, the organization experienced:

- Streamlined budgeting and forecasting processes.

- Improved accuracy in predicting sales and expenses.

- Reduced manual data entry errors.

Case Study 3: Expense Analysis for Non-profit

Background:

- A non-profit organization needed to optimize its expenses to allocate resources efficiently.

Solution:

- Power BI was employed to analyze expense data. The reports helped identify areas where cost savings could be achieved without compromising the organization's mission.

Benefits:

- With Power BI, the non-profit:

  - Analyzed expense data more effectively.

  - Optimized resource allocation.

  - Demonstrated financial transparency to donors and stakeholders.

Case Study 4: Audit and Compliance Reporting

Background:

- An auditing firm required a tool to streamline its audit process and create compliance reports for clients.

Solution:

- Power BI was used to design customized audit and compliance reports. These reports automated data collection, analysis, and report generation.

Benefits:

  - With Power BI, the auditing firm:

    - Improved audit efficiency.

    - Enhanced client service by providing real-time insights.

    - Ensured compliance with industry regulations.

These case studies demonstrate the versatility of Power BI in addressing financial and accounting challenges. The platform's ability to integrate data, provide real-time insights, and simplify reporting processes has led to substantial improvements in efficiency, decision-making, and financial transparency for organizations across different sectors.

Best Practices and Tips for Real-world Implementation

When implementing Power BI for financial reporting and accounting, following best practices and tips can make a significant difference in the success of your projects. Here, we provide guidance on how to effectively deploy Power BI in real-world scenarios for finance and accounting.

* Understand Your Data:

  - Before diving into Power BI, ensure a deep understanding of your data sources. Recognize the data quality, structure, and potential challenges in your financial data.

* Data Modeling:

  - Invest time in data modeling. Create a well-structured data model that accurately represents your financial data. Define relationships between tables and create measures that are crucial for financial analysis.

* Data Security:

  - Pay close attention to data security. Ensure that sensitive financial data is appropriately protected. Use Power BI's security features to control access to financial reports.

* Automated Data Refresh:

  - Schedule data refresh at regular intervals to keep reports up-to-date. Be mindful of any dependencies in your data sources, and set up data refresh accordingly.

* Visualization Best Practices:

  - When creating financial reports, choose the right visualization types. Bar and line charts are useful for time-series data, while tables or matrices are excellent for displaying detailed financial information.

* Use DAX Effectively:

- Master Data Analysis Expressions (DAX). DAX is essential for creating calculations and measures for financial reports. Optimize your DAX formulas for performance.

* Collaboration and Sharing:

- Develop a well-defined collaboration and sharing strategy. Determine who needs access to financial reports and create secure sharing channels within Power BI.

* Regular Training:

- Invest in training for your team. Regularly update your knowledge on Power BI features and best practices to stay current.

* Version Control:

- Implement version control for your Power BI reports. This ensures that changes are tracked, and you can revert to previous versions if needed.

* Documentation:

- Document your Power BI reports comprehensively. This includes data source information, data model details, report definitions, and usage guidelines.

* Monitoring and Maintenance:

- Set up monitoring for your financial reports. Regularly check for data anomalies, errors, or disruptions in data refresh. Develop a maintenance plan for ongoing support.

* User Feedback:

- Collect feedback from end-users. Understand their requirements, pain points, and suggestions for improvements. Use this feedback to iterate and enhance your reports.

* Scalability:

   - Plan for scalability. As your organization grows, your reporting needs may change. Ensure that your Power BI solution can adapt to evolving requirements.

* Compliance:

   - Be aware of industry-specific compliance and regulatory requirements. Ensure that your financial reports comply with relevant standards.

* Real-time Reporting:

   - Consider implementing real-time reporting for critical financial data. Power BI supports streaming datasets for this purpose.

By following these best practices and tips, you can ensure the successful implementation of Power BI in the finance and accounting domain. Power BI has the potential to unlock valuable financial insights, streamline reporting processes, and drive data-driven decision-making in your organization.

CHAPTER V
Mastering Power BI for Finance

5.1 Advanced DAX Formulas for Finance

Complex Calculations and Formulas

In finance, the need for complex calculations and formulas is prevalent, whether you're dealing with investment analysis, risk management, or financial modeling. Power BI provides a robust platform for handling these intricate financial calculations, and mastering the use of complex DAX formulas is crucial.

* Understanding Complex Calculations:

   - Complex financial calculations often involve multiple variables, conditional logic, and iterative processes. Before diving into DAX, ensure you have a clear understanding of the financial concept you're trying to model.

* Iterative Functions in DAX:

   - DAX provides iterative functions like `SUMX`, `AVERAGEX`, and `FILTER`. These are invaluable for performing calculations that involve iterating through rows in a table. For example, calculating a moving average or cumulative totals.

* Time Intelligence Functions:

   - Finance frequently requires time-based calculations. DAX's time intelligence functions like `TOTALYTD`, `SAMEPERIODLASTYEAR`, and `DATESYTD` are essential for handling scenarios such as year-to-date comparisons and seasonal analysis.

* Advanced IF Statements:

   - Complex calculations often involve conditional logic. Advanced `IF` statements using functions like `SWITCH` can help manage intricate conditions.

* Parameter Tables:

   - Parameter tables can be used to store variables and inputs for complex calculations. For instance, storing interest rates, growth rates, or thresholds in a separate table can make your DAX formulas more adaptable.

* Custom Functions (Measures):

   - Create custom DAX measures for complex calculations. These measures can encapsulate intricate logic, making your formulas more readable and reusable.

* Handling Circular Dependencies:

   - In financial models, circular dependencies may arise. Learn how to manage these situations by using DAX functions like `EARLIER` and `FILTER`.

* Scenario Analysis:

   - Financial modeling often involves scenario analysis. Implement techniques for handling multiple scenarios by using slicers and parameters to dynamically switch between different assumptions.

* Integration with Power Query:

   - In some cases, it may be more efficient to perform complex calculations in Power Query before loading data into the data model. Understand when and how to leverage Power Query for financial transformations.

* Performance Optimization:

- Complex calculations can impact report performance. Learn how to optimize DAX formulas for faster execution, such as using summarization and aggregation.

* Real-world Examples:

- To solidify your understanding, work through real-world examples. Create DAX measures for calculating net present value (NPV), internal rate of return (IRR), option pricing models, or any other financial metrics relevant to your organization.

* Testing and Validation:

- Rigorously test and validate your complex calculations. Verify that the results align with your expectations and business requirements.

Incorporating complex calculations and formulas into your Power BI financial reports empowers you to derive deeper insights and support critical financial decision-making. Mastering these techniques will give you a competitive edge in the field of finance and accounting.

This section provides comprehensive guidance on handling complex financial calculations and formulas in Power BI. If you have specific questions or need further details on any of these topics, please feel free to ask.

Performance Optimization Techniques

Optimizing the performance of your Power BI reports is essential to ensure fast and responsive dashboards. This is particularly crucial when dealing with large financial datasets and complex calculations. In this section, we'll explore various techniques for enhancing report performance.

* Data Model Optimization:

- Start by optimizing your data model. Remove unnecessary columns, tables, or relationships that aren't used in your reports. Keeping the model clean and efficient is the foundation for good performance.

* Use Summarization and Aggregation:

 - When working with large datasets, use aggregation functions (SUM, AVERAGE, COUNT, etc.) to summarize data at higher levels of granularity. This reduces the amount of data loaded into memory and speeds up query execution.

* Manage Relationships Efficiently:

 - Ensure your relationships between tables are correctly defined and don't create circular dependencies. Use bi-directional filtering only when necessary, as it can impact performance.

* Minimize the Use of DAX Variables:

 - While DAX variables can improve code readability, excessive use of variables can lead to slower performance. Use them judiciously, and consider the impact on query folding.

* Filter Context Optimization:

 - Be mindful of the number of filters in your report. Complex slicers or filters applied to many visuals can slow down performance. Use slicers and filters selectively.

* Query Folding:

 - Leverage query folding, which pushes some operations back to the data source, such as SQL Server or Power Query. It reduces the amount of data transferred to Power BI and can significantly speed up your reports.

* Optimize DAX Measures:

- Review your DAX measures for efficiency. Avoid using functions like ALL, FILTER, and CALCULATETABLE excessively, as they can slow down calculations.

* Data Compression:

- Power BI employs data compression techniques. Utilize these to reduce the size of your data model. The smaller the model, the faster the performance.

* Use DirectQuery or Live Connection:

- For extremely large datasets, consider using DirectQuery or Live Connection mode to maintain a connection to the data source. This can offload processing to the source system.

* Distribute Workload:

- Distribute your data processing and calculations between the data source, Power Query, and DAX as appropriate. Balance the workload to optimize performance.

* Performance Profiling:

- Use Power BI's built-in performance analyzer and query profiler to identify bottlenecks and slow-performing visuals. Address these issues iteratively.

* Hardware Considerations:

- Ensure that your hardware meets the requirements for running Power BI. A slow machine can affect report rendering.

* Report Design Best Practices:

- Adhere to best practices in report design. Use appropriate visuals and layouts. Avoid using too many visuals on a single page, as it can degrade performance.

Optimizing report performance is an ongoing process. Regularly test and refine your reports to ensure they meet the needs of your financial users. By employing these performance optimization techniques, you'll deliver snappy and responsive financial reports in Power BI.

Practical DAX Examples

Data Analysis Expressions (DAX) is a powerful formula language used in Power BI to create custom calculations and aggregations for your financial reports. In this section, we'll explore practical DAX examples tailored for finance professionals. Each example comes with detailed steps and explanations.

* Calculating Year-to-Date (YTD) Totals:

   - Often in finance, you need to calculate YTD totals for metrics like revenue, expenses, or profits. Learn how to create a DAX measure to dynamically calculate YTD totals based on the selected date in your report.

* Forecasting Future Values:

   - Financial forecasting is essential. We'll walk you through building DAX measures that use historical data to predict future values, such as sales or cash flow, using techniques like moving averages or exponential smoothing.

* Calculating Financial Ratios:

   - Finance professionals frequently need to compute financial ratios like liquidity ratios, profitability ratios, and leverage ratios. We'll demonstrate how to create DAX measures to calculate these ratios in your Power BI report.

* Creating Rolling Averages:

   - Rolling averages are useful for smoothing out fluctuations in financial data. You'll learn how to build DAX measures that calculate rolling averages for metrics like monthly sales or quarterly expenses.

* Variance Analysis:

- DAX can be used to perform variance analysis, helping you compare actual vs. budget or actual vs. previous periods. We'll guide you through creating DAX measures that display these variances.

* Top N Analysis:

- Finance professionals often want to focus on the top-performing or underperforming entities. You'll discover how to use DAX to perform Top N analysis for metrics like top customers, products, or regions.

* Time-Intelligence Functions:

- DAX offers a range of time-intelligence functions. We'll show you how to leverage functions like TOTALYTD, SAMEPERIODLASTYEAR, and DATESYTD to gain insights into your financial data.

* Handling Currency Conversion:

- When dealing with international finances, you might need to perform currency conversion. We'll provide examples of how DAX can help you handle multi-currency reporting in your Power BI dashboards.

Each practical example is illustrated with step-by-step instructions and DAX code snippets. You'll gain the skills needed to create custom DAX measures tailored to your specific financial reporting requirements, making your Power BI reports more insightful and relevant for financial   analysis.

5.2 Financial Planning and Budgeting

Building Budgeting Models in Power BI

Effective financial planning and budgeting are crucial for organizations to manage their resources and make informed decisions. Power BI provides a powerful platform for building budgeting models, and in this section, we will explore how to create comprehensive budgeting models using Power BI. Below is a step-by-step guide on building budgeting models:

Step 1: Data Preparation

  - The first step in building a budgeting model in Power BI is data preparation. Ensure that you have your historical financial data available in a format that can be loaded into Power BI. This data should include historical revenues, expenses, and other financial metrics.

Step 2: Data Import

  - Use Power Query in Power BI to import your historical financial data. You may need to transform and clean the data, remove any outliers, and ensure that it's structured correctly for budgeting.

Step 3: Budget Assumptions

  - Define your budget assumptions, including revenue growth rates, expense projections, and other factors that influence your budget. You can create a separate table to store these assumptions.

Step 4: Budget Formulas

  - Develop DAX formulas to calculate the budgeted values based on your assumptions. You'll use DAX to forecast future revenues, expenses, and profits.

Step 5: Budget Tables and Relationships

- Create budget tables and establish relationships between historical data and budget data. This ensures that your budget calculations are tied to historical trends.

Step 6: Visualizing the Budget

- Design interactive Power BI reports that display historical and budgeted financial data. You can use visualizations like line charts, bar charts, and tables to present the budget alongside actual results.

Step 7: Budget vs. Actual Analysis

- Implement budget vs. actual analysis by calculating variances and visualizing them in your reports. This helps in identifying where the actual results deviate from the budget.

Step 8: Data Entry and What-If Analysis

- For more advanced budgeting models, you can create data entry forms and enable what-if analysis in Power BI, allowing users to adjust budget assumptions and instantly see the impact on financial projections.

Step 9: Monitoring and Reporting

- Use Power BI's scheduled data refresh to ensure your budgeting model stays up to date. Create reports and dashboards that provide an overview of the budgeting process and results.

Step 10: Collaborative Budgeting

- Utilize Power BI's collaboration features to enable multiple team members to collaborate on the budgeting process, making it more efficient and collaborative.

By following these steps and leveraging the capabilities of Power BI, you can build robust and interactive budgeting models for your organization. This empowers you to make data-driven budgeting decisions and monitor your financial performance effectively.

Variance Analysis and Forecasting

Variance analysis is a critical component of financial planning and budgeting, helping organizations understand the differences between budgeted (forecasted) and actual financial performance. Power BI can assist in performing variance analysis and forecasting effectively. In this section, we'll explore how to conduct variance analysis and forecasting in Power BI.

Step 1: Data Integration

- Begin by importing both your historical financial data and budget data into Power BI. Ensure the data is appropriately structured for analysis.

Step 2: Data Modeling

- Create relationships between your historical and budget data tables. Power BI's Data Analysis Expressions (DAX) language will be instrumental in performing calculations for variance analysis.

Step 3: Calculating Variances

- Use DAX formulas to calculate variances between actual and budgeted figures. Common variance calculations include Revenue Variance, Expense Variance, and Profit Variance. For example, the formula for Revenue Variance might be:

```

Revenue Variance = SUM('Budget Data'[Budgeted Revenue]) - SUM('Actual Data'[Actual Revenue])

```

Repeat this for different types of expenses as well.

Step 4: Visualizing Variances

- Design reports and dashboards that illustrate variances using visualizations like tables, charts, and KPI cards. Utilize Power BI's conditional formatting to highlight positive or negative variances.

Step 5: Forecasting

- Power BI provides several methods for forecasting, such as exponential smoothing or time series analysis. Use these forecasting techniques to extend your budget data into the future based on historical trends.

Step 6: Scenario Analysis

- Create "what-if" scenarios by adjusting key assumptions in your budget, and visualize the impact on variances and forecasts in real-time. This enables proactive decision-making based on different scenarios.

Step 7: Monitoring

- Set up alerts and automated reports to monitor variances and forecasts regularly. This keeps stakeholders informed about the financial performance relative to the budget.

Step 8: Collaboration

- Leverage Power BI's collaboration features to share budget variances and forecasts with relevant stakeholders for discussion and decision-making.

Variance analysis and forecasting in Power BI provide a dynamic approach to assessing financial performance against budgeted expectations and making necessary adjustments. It empowers finance and accounting professionals to identify trends, respond to changes, and make informed decisions.

5.3 Regulatory Compliance and Audit Reporting

Meeting Regulatory Requirements with Power BI

Meeting regulatory requirements is a crucial aspect of financial reporting for many organizations, especially those in highly regulated industries such as finance and healthcare. Power BI provides powerful tools to help you meet these requirements efficiently. In this section, we will explore how to leverage Power BI to ensure regulatory compliance.

Step 1: Identify Regulatory Requirements

- Start by clearly identifying the specific regulatory requirements that your organization needs to adhere to. This may include reporting standards like GAAP, IFRS, or industry-specific regulations.

Step 2: Data Collection and Integration

- Ensure that you have access to all the necessary financial data required for compliance. Integrate data sources and create a centralized data model in Power BI.

Step 3: Data Validation

- Implement data validation rules and checks to ensure the accuracy and integrity of your financial data. Power BI's DAX language can be used to perform these checks.

Step 4: Report Design

- Design your financial reports in Power BI to comply with regulatory standards. Use visualizations that make it easy to understand complex financial data and ensure that the reports include all the required disclosures.

Step 5: Documentation

- Keep comprehensive documentation of your reports, data sources, and calculations. This documentation is essential for audit and compliance purposes.

Step 6: Audit Trails

- Implement audit trails and tracking mechanisms to monitor any changes made to the reports or data. This ensures data integrity and transparency.

Step 7: Automation

- Use Power BI's automation features to schedule and distribute compliance reports to relevant stakeholders on a regular basis.

Step 8: External Audits

- Prepare for external audits by ensuring that your Power BI reports and data are easily accessible to auditors. Power BI's export and sharing capabilities are valuable for this step.

Step 9: Version Control

- Maintain version control of your reports, ensuring that you can access previous versions and track changes over time.

Step 10: Continuous Monitoring

- Continuously monitor your compliance reports and make necessary updates as regulatory requirements change. This ensures that your organization remains in compliance.

Power BI's flexibility, data modeling capabilities, and automation features can significantly streamline the process of meeting regulatory requirements. It provides a transparent and auditable platform for financial reporting, making it easier to demonstrate compliance to auditors and regulators.

Preparing for Audits and Compliance Reporting

Preparing for audits and compliance reporting is a critical aspect of financial governance and transparency for organizations in regulated industries. This section will guide you through the steps to effectively prepare for audits and ensure compliance using Power BI.

Step 1: Define Audit Objectives

- Start by clearly defining the objectives of the audit. Understand the specific areas and data that auditors will examine. This helps you focus your efforts on the most critical aspects.

Step 2: Data Preparation

- Ensure that your financial data in Power BI is well-organized and up-to-date. Verify the accuracy of data sources and perform data cleaning and transformation if necessary.

Step 3: Documentation

- Maintain comprehensive documentation of your Power BI reports and data sources. Documentation should include data definitions, report details, and any custom calculations or measures.

Step 4: Data Security

- Implement robust data security measures within Power BI to ensure that sensitive financial data is accessible only to authorized personnel. Power BI offers role-level security for this purpose.

Step 5: Compliance Checks

- Use Power BI to run compliance checks, automated validation, and calculations to ensure that financial data complies with regulatory standards. Implement DAX formulas and measures for these checks.

Step 6: Report Validation

- Thoroughly validate your financial reports to ensure that they accurately reflect the financial data and meet the reporting standards. Double-check for any discrepancies or inconsistencies.

Step 7: Accessibility

- Ensure that the audit team has appropriate access to your Power BI reports and data during the audit process. Share reports securely and make data accessible for auditors.

Step 8: Audit Trails

- Enable audit trails and tracking mechanisms within Power BI to record any changes made to reports or data during the audit. This provides transparency and a detailed history.

Step 9: Testing

- Perform mock audits or internal audits to identify any potential issues or areas of concern. This allows you to address issues before the external audit.

Step 10: Compliance Reporting

- Use Power BI to generate compliance reports that provide an overview of your organization's adherence to regulatory standards. These reports should be easily understandable by auditors.

Step 11: Auditors' Requirements

- Collaborate with the audit team to understand their specific requirements and data they need for the audit. Provide any necessary documentation and guidance.

Step 12: Continuous Improvement

- After the audit, conduct a post-audit review to identify areas for improvement. Make any necessary enhancements to your Power BI reports and processes for future audits.

Power BI's capabilities in data modeling, report design, and automation are instrumental in preparing for audits and ensuring compliance. By following these steps, you can streamline the audit process and demonstrate that your organization is committed to financial transparency and compliance with regulatory standards.

CHAPTER VI
Advanced Analytics and Future Trends in Finance with Power BI

6.1 Predictive Analytics for Financial Forecasting

Introduction to Predictive Analytics

Predictive analytics is a powerful tool that leverages historical data and statistical algorithms to make informed predictions about future trends, behaviors, and outcomes. In the context of financial and accounting, predictive analytics plays a crucial role in forecasting financial metrics, identifying potential risks, and optimizing decision-making. This section will provide a detailed introduction to predictive analytics and its application within Power BI for financial forecasting.

Understanding Predictive Analytics

Predictive analytics involves using historical data to build predictive models that can help forecast future events or trends. It is based on the idea that past patterns and data can be used to make educated guesses about what might happen in the future. In the world of finance and accounting, predictive analytics can be used for various purposes:

1. Financial Forecasting: Predict future revenue, expenses, and other financial metrics to make budgeting and strategic planning more accurate.

2. Risk Assessment: Identify potential financial risks, such as defaulting on loans or investment losses, by analyzing historical data and market conditions.

3. Customer Behavior Prediction: Understand customer behavior by predicting purchasing trends and preferences.

4. Fraud Detection: Detect unusual patterns or anomalies in financial transactions that may indicate fraudulent activity.

Steps to Implement Predictive Analytics in Power BI

To implement predictive analytics in Power BI, follow these steps:

1. Data Preparation: Start by collecting and cleaning historical data relevant to your analysis. This data may include financial records, market data, customer information, and other relevant variables.

2. Data Exploration: Explore the data to gain insights into its characteristics, trends, and potential predictors. Visualization tools in Power BI can be helpful for this step.

3. Feature Selection: Identify the features (variables) that are most likely to influence the predictive model. This step involves data analysis and domain knowledge.

4. Model Selection: Choose the appropriate predictive model based on your analysis goals. Power BI supports various modeling techniques, including linear regression, time series forecasting, and machine learning models.

5. Training the Model: Use historical data to train the selected predictive model. Power BI provides tools to split data into training and testing sets.

6. Model Evaluation: Assess the accuracy and performance of the model using evaluation metrics such as Mean Absolute Error (MAE) or Root Mean Squared Error (RMSE). Make necessary adjustments to improve the model.

7. Prediction: Once the model is trained and validated, use it to make predictions about future financial or accounting trends.

Example: Time Series Forecasting

Time series forecasting is a common predictive analytics technique in finance. It involves making predictions based on time-ordered data, such as stock prices, sales figures, or financial reports. Here's a simple example of how to perform time series forecasting in Power BI:

1. Data Import: Import historical time series data into Power BI, ensuring it includes a date/time column and the relevant financial metrics.

2. Data Exploration: Create visualizations to explore the time series data, identifying trends, seasonality, and any irregular patterns.

3. Model Selection: Choose a time series forecasting model, such as ARIMA (AutoRegressive Integrated Moving Average) or Exponential Smoothing, based on the characteristics of the data.

4. Model Training: Use the historical data to train the selected model. Power BI provides built-in functions for time series forecasting.

5. Model Evaluation: Evaluate the model's performance using metrics like Mean Absolute Percentage Error (MAPE) or Mean Absolute Error (MAE).

6. Prediction: Apply the trained model to make future predictions, creating forecasts for the financial metrics of interest.

Power BI's integration with R and Python also allows for more advanced predictive modeling using custom scripts and machine learning algorithms.

Conclusion

Predictive analytics is a valuable tool for finance and accounting professionals, enabling them to make data-driven decisions and gain insights into future financial trends and risks. Power BI's capabilities for data analysis, modeling, and visualization make it a powerful platform for implementing predictive analytics in the financial sector. By following the steps outlined above and leveraging Power BI's features, you can unlock valuable financial insights and improve your organization's financial forecasting accuracy.

Time Series Forecasting in Power BI

Time series forecasting is a critical component of financial analysis in Power BI. It allows you to make predictions about future financial trends based on historical time-ordered data. Whether you want to forecast stock prices, sales figures, or budgeting data, understanding how to perform time series forecasting in Power BI is essential. In this section, we'll provide a detailed guide on how to conduct time series forecasting using Power BI, including step-by-step instructions and code examples where necessary.

Understanding Time Series Forecasting

Time series forecasting involves making predictions about future values of a variable based on its past values and the assumption that the underlying patterns will continue. In finance and accounting, this can be applied to various scenarios, such as forecasting future stock prices, sales, or budgeting data. Power BI offers tools and functionalities to perform time series forecasting effectively.

Steps to Perform Time Series Forecasting in Power BI

Follow these steps to perform time series forecasting in Power BI:

1. Data Preparation: Import historical time-ordered data into Power BI. Ensure that your dataset includes a date/time column and the relevant numerical variable you want to forecast, such as sales figures.

2. Data Exploration: Create visualizations and plots to understand the historical time series data. Identify trends, seasonality, and any outliers.

3. Model Selection: Choose the appropriate time series forecasting model based on the characteristics of your data. Common models include ARIMA (AutoRegressive Integrated Moving Average), Exponential Smoothing, and seasonal decomposition.

4. Model Training: Split your data into training and testing datasets. Use the training data to build and fine-tune your forecasting model. Power BI provides built-in functions and visuals for this purpose.

5. Model Evaluation: Evaluate the accuracy of your model using appropriate metrics. Common metrics include Mean Absolute Error (MAE), Mean Squared Error (MSE), and Root Mean Squared Error (RMSE).

6. Forecasting: Apply your trained model to make forecasts for future periods. You can use DAX functions and visuals in Power BI to generate these forecasts.

Example: Time Series Forecasting in Power BI

Let's illustrate the steps with a simple example of time series forecasting in Power BI. We'll use a sample dataset containing historical monthly sales data.

1. Data Preparation: Import your dataset into Power BI. Ensure it includes a "Date" column and a "Sales" column.

2. Data Exploration: Create line charts or time series visualizations to explore your sales data. Identify any trends, seasonality, or outliers.

3. Model Selection: Based on your data exploration, you might choose to apply an Exponential Smoothing model to capture both trend and seasonality.

4. Model Training: Split your data into a training set and a testing set, usually by selecting a specific time period for testing. For instance, you can use the first 80% of your data for training.

5. Model Evaluation: Train your Exponential Smoothing model on the training set and evaluate its performance using RMSE.

6. Forecasting: Apply the trained model to your entire dataset to generate forecasts for future sales. You can use DAX functions like `FORECAST.ETS()` to do this.

```DAX
```

```
ForecastedSales =

FORECAST.ETS(

    Sales,

    <your dataset>,

    <your date column>,

    12,    // Number of periods to forecast (e.g., 12 for one year)

    "AAN"   // Seasonality parameters (A: Additive, A: Additive, N: No seasonality)

)
```

This code generates a forecast of sales for the next 12 periods with additive seasonality.

Conclusion

Time series forecasting in Power BI is a valuable tool for financial professionals and accountants to make data-driven predictions about future financial trends. By following the steps outlined above and leveraging Power BI's built-in functions and visuals, you can effectively perform time series forecasting and gain insights into your financial data, helping you make informed decisions and accurate forecasts.

Predictive Models for Budgeting

Predictive models are a valuable asset in the field of finance and accounting, particularly when it comes to budgeting. These models use historical data and statistical algorithms to forecast future financial outcomes, helping organizations make more accurate and data-driven budgeting decisions. In this section, we will delve into the specifics of building predictive models for budgeting using Power BI, providing step-by-step instructions and code examples where relevant.

Understanding Predictive Models for Budgeting

Predictive models for budgeting leverage historical financial data to predict future financial metrics and guide budget planning. These models can be applied to a wide range of budgeting scenarios, including revenue projections, expense forecasting, and cash flow management. By incorporating predictive models into the budgeting process, organizations can make more informed financial decisions.

Steps to Build Predictive Models for Budgeting in Power BI

Follow these steps to build predictive models for budgeting in Power BI:

1. Data Preparation: Collect and clean historical financial data, ensuring it includes the relevant variables for your budgeting scenario, such as revenue, expenses, and time periods.

2. Data Exploration: Explore the historical data to understand the trends, patterns, and any potential predictors that can influence your budgeting model.

3. Model Selection: Choose an appropriate predictive model for your budgeting needs. Common models include linear regression, time series forecasting, and machine learning models.

4. Data Splitting: Divide the historical data into two parts: a training dataset and a testing dataset. The training dataset will be used to build and fine-tune the predictive model.

5. Model Training: Train the selected predictive model using the training dataset. Fine-tune the model parameters to optimize its performance.

6. Model Evaluation: Assess the accuracy and performance of the model using appropriate evaluation metrics such as Mean Absolute Error (MAE) or Root Mean Squared Error (RMSE).

7. Budget Projections: Apply the trained model to make budget projections for future periods. These projections will be based on the historical data and the insights gained from the model.

Example: Linear Regression for Revenue Budgeting

Let's illustrate the steps with a simple example of using linear regression for revenue budgeting in Power BI:

1. Data Preparation: Import historical data into Power BI, including columns for "Year," "Month," and "Revenue."

2. Data Exploration: Create visualizations to explore the historical revenue data, looking for trends and seasonality.

3. Model Selection: Choose linear regression as the predictive model for revenue budgeting. It assumes a linear relationship between time and revenue.

4. Data Splitting: Split the data into a training dataset (e.g., the first 80% of the data) and a testing dataset (the remaining 20%).

5. Model Training: Use Power BI's linear regression modeling features to train the model using the training dataset. Adjust model parameters as needed.

6. Model Evaluation: Evaluate the model's performance using metrics like RMSE to assess the accuracy of revenue predictions.

7. Budget Projections: Apply the trained linear regression model to forecast revenue for future months or years based on the historical data.

```DAX
ProjectedRevenue =

VAR RegressionModel =

    REGRESS(

        'Budgeting Data'[Revenue],

        'Budgeting Data'[Year],

        'Budgeting Data'[Month]

    )

RETURN

    ADDCOLUMNS(

        'Budgeting Data',

        "PredictedRevenue",

        IF(ISBLANK(RegressionModel), BLANK(), RegressionModel)

    )
```

This DAX formula uses the `REGRESS` function to create a linear regression model and predict future revenue based on the 'Year' and 'Month' columns.

Conclusion

Predictive models for budgeting in Power BI provide finance and accounting professionals with a powerful tool to make data-driven budgeting decisions. By following the steps outlined above and leveraging Power BI's features, you can effectively build predictive models to improve the accuracy of your budgeting process. These models enable organizations to plan their financial resources more efficiently and make informed budgeting decisions.

6.2 Machine Learning Applications in Finance

Machine Learning Fundamentals

Machine learning has become a powerful tool in the field of finance, enabling organizations to extract valuable insights from large datasets, make data-driven decisions, and automate various financial tasks. In this section, we'll delve into the fundamentals of machine learning, explaining key concepts, providing real-world examples, and outlining the steps to implement machine learning in finance using Power BI.

Understanding Machine Learning Fundamentals

Machine learning is a subset of artificial intelligence that focuses on developing algorithms that can learn from data and make predictions or decisions without being explicitly programmed. In finance, machine learning can be applied to a wide range of tasks, including risk assessment, fraud detection, credit scoring, investment strategies, and customer behavior analysis.

Key Concepts in Machine Learning

1. Data: Data is the foundation of machine learning. In finance, this can include historical financial data, customer transaction records, market data, and more. The quality and quantity of data are critical factors in machine learning success.

2. Features and Labels: Features are the input variables used by a machine learning model to make predictions. Labels are the target variables that the model aims to predict. For example, in credit scoring, features might include credit history, income, and age, while the label is the likelihood of loan default.

3. Training and Testing Data: To build a machine learning model, data is typically divided into a training dataset used to train the model and a testing dataset used to evaluate its performance. This helps assess how well the model generalizes to new, unseen data.

4. Algorithms: Machine learning algorithms are mathematical models that learn from data. Common algorithms in finance include decision trees, random forests, support vector machines, and neural networks.

5. Supervised vs. Unsupervised Learning: In supervised learning, the model is trained on labeled data. In unsupervised learning, the model identifies patterns or clusters in unlabeled data.

Steps to Implement Machine Learning in Finance with Power BI

1. Data Collection: Gather and prepare relevant financial data for your machine learning project. Ensure data quality and completeness.

2. Data Preprocessing: Clean and preprocess the data. This may involve handling missing values, scaling features, and encoding categorical variables.

3. Data Splitting: Divide the data into a training set and a testing set. Typically, 70-80% of the data is used for training, and the rest is used for testing.

4. Model Selection: Choose an appropriate machine learning algorithm based on your specific finance task. For example, if you're building a credit scoring model, you might opt for a decision tree or logistic regression.

5. Model Training: Train the selected model on the training data. The model learns to make predictions by finding patterns in the data.

6. Model Evaluation: Evaluate the model's performance on the testing data using relevant metrics. For credit scoring, metrics like accuracy, precision, recall, and the ROC-AUC curve are common.

7. Deployment: Once the model is satisfactory, deploy it within your Power BI reports or dashboards to make real-time predictions or automate financial processes.

Real-world Example: Credit Scoring

Let's take a real-world example of credit scoring, a common application of machine learning in finance. Credit scoring models predict the creditworthiness of applicants based on their financial history and other factors.

1. Data Collection: Gather historical credit data, including applicant information, credit history, income, and loan outcomes.

2. Data Preprocessing: Clean the data by handling missing values and encoding categorical variables (e.g., employment status).

3. Data Splitting: Divide the data into training and testing sets.

4. Model Selection: Choose a machine learning algorithm, such as a logistic regression model.

5. Model Training: Train the logistic regression model on the training data.

6. Model Evaluation: Assess the model's performance on the testing data, obtaining metrics like accuracy, precision, recall, and the ROC-AUC curve.

7. Deployment: Integrate the trained credit scoring model into Power BI to assess the creditworthiness of loan applicants in real-time.

Conclusion

Machine learning fundamentals are essential for finance professionals seeking to leverage the power of data-driven decision-making. By understanding the key concepts and following the steps outlined above, you can successfully implement machine learning in finance using Power BI. This enables you to automate tasks, make more accurate predictions, and gain valuable insights from your financial data.

Credit Scoring Models

Credit scoring models play a pivotal role in the finance industry, helping organizations assess the creditworthiness of individuals and businesses. By using historical financial data, these models can predict the likelihood of loan defaults and assist in making informed lending decisions. In this section, we will explore credit scoring models in detail, provide concrete examples, and outline the steps to implement credit scoring models using Power BI.

Understanding Credit Scoring Models

Credit scoring models are statistical models designed to evaluate an applicant's creditworthiness. They assign a numerical score to an individual or business based on their financial history, behaviors, and other relevant factors. The higher the credit score, the more creditworthy the applicant is considered. These models are widely used by banks, lenders, and financial institutions to make lending decisions.

Key Components of Credit Scoring Models

1. Credit Data: This includes historical financial data, such as credit history, outstanding debts, payment history, and personal information.

2. Credit Score: The output of a credit scoring model is a credit score, which quantifies an applicant's creditworthiness.

3. Thresholds: Lenders establish specific credit score thresholds to determine whether an applicant qualifies for a loan or credit.

4. Predictive Variables: Credit scoring models use predictive variables like income, employment status, and previous loan history to assess credit risk.

Steps to Implement Credit Scoring Models in Power BI

To implement credit scoring models in Power BI, follow these steps:

1. Data Collection: Gather historical credit data, including applicant information and their credit history. This data serves as the foundation of your model.

2. Data Preprocessing: Clean and preprocess the data. Handle missing values, scale features, and encode categorical variables.

3. Data Splitting: Divide the data into a training set and a testing set. The training set is used to build the credit scoring model.

4. Model Selection: Choose an appropriate credit scoring model, such as logistic regression, decision trees, or random forests.

5. Model Training: Train the selected model using the training data. The model learns to make predictions based on the applicant's financial data.

6. Model Evaluation: Evaluate the model's performance on the testing data using metrics like accuracy, precision, recall, and the ROC-AUC curve.

7. Deployment: Deploy the trained credit scoring model within Power BI to assess the creditworthiness of loan applicants in real-time.

Real-world Example: Credit Scoring with Logistic Regression

Let's walk through a real-world example of credit scoring using logistic regression, a common machine learning algorithm for this purpose:

1. Data Collection: Collect historical credit data that includes applicant information, credit history, and loan outcomes.

2. Data Preprocessing: Clean the data, handle missing values, and encode categorical variables like employment status.

3. Data Splitting: Split the data into a training set (e.g., 80% of the data) and a testing set (20%).

4. Model Selection: Choose logistic regression as the credit scoring model. Logistic regression models the probability of loan default.

5. Model Training: Train the logistic regression model on the training data. The model learns to predict the likelihood of loan default based on applicant features.

6. Model Evaluation: Evaluate the model's performance using metrics like accuracy, precision, recall, and the ROC-AUC curve on the testing data.

7. Deployment: Embed the trained logistic regression model within Power BI to assess the creditworthiness of loan applicants in real-time.

Conclusion

Credit scoring models are essential tools in the finance industry, enabling organizations to make informed lending decisions. By understanding the key components and following the steps outlined above, you can successfully implement credit scoring models in Power BI. These models help automate the lending process, reduce risk, and improve the accuracy of credit assessments, ultimately benefiting both lenders and borrowers.

Fraud Detection and Prevention

Fraud detection and prevention are critical components of financial security in today's digital age. With the increasing prevalence of online transactions, organizations face a growing need to protect themselves and their customers from fraudulent activities. In this section, we will explore the intricacies of fraud detection and prevention using Power BI, offering detailed insights, real-world examples, and a step-by-step guide on implementing fraud detection systems.

Understanding Fraud Detection and Prevention

Fraud detection and prevention are processes that aim to identify and mitigate fraudulent activities before they cause financial harm. These activities can encompass various forms of fraud, such as credit card fraud, identity theft, insurance fraud, and more. In the financial sector, it's essential to have robust systems and models in place to detect and prevent fraud.

Key Concepts in Fraud Detection

1. Anomaly Detection: This approach identifies irregular patterns or anomalies in data that may indicate fraudulent behavior. Anomalies can be identified through statistical analysis, machine learning, or rule-based systems.

2. Machine Learning Models: Machine learning plays a crucial role in fraud detection. Models, such as decision trees, neural networks, and logistic regression, can be trained on historical data to recognize patterns associated with fraud.

3. Data Sources: Data for fraud detection can be sourced from various channels, including transaction records, user activity logs, and external data feeds.

4. Scoring and Alerts: After analyzing the data, a fraud detection system assigns scores to transactions or activities, indicating the likelihood of fraud. High-risk transactions trigger alerts for further investigation.

Steps to Implement Fraud Detection and Prevention in Power BI

To establish a fraud detection and prevention system in Power BI, follow these steps:

1. Data Collection: Gather relevant data, including transaction records, user activities, and any other data sources that may contain information related to fraudulent behavior.

2. Data Preprocessing: Clean and preprocess the data. This may involve handling missing values, scaling features, and encoding categorical variables.

3. Anomaly Detection: Employ anomaly detection techniques, such as statistical analysis, to identify irregular patterns in the data. Alternatively, use machine learning models like isolation forests or one-class SVM.

4. Model Training: Train machine learning models to recognize patterns associated with fraud. Utilize labeled data where possible to teach the model about historical fraud cases.

5. Scoring and Alerts: Assign scores to transactions or activities based on the likelihood of fraud. Define threshold values that trigger alerts for high-risk transactions.

6. Model Evaluation: Assess the performance of your fraud detection system using metrics like precision, recall, and the F1 score. Fine-tune the system to minimize false positives and false negatives.

7. Deployment: Integrate the fraud detection and prevention system into Power BI reports or dashboards, where it can provide real-time monitoring and alerts.

Real-world Example: Credit Card Fraud Detection

Let's illustrate the steps with a real-world example of credit card fraud detection, a common application of fraud detection in the financial sector:

1. Data Collection: Collect historical credit card transaction data, including transaction amounts, merchant information, and transaction timestamps.

2. Data Preprocessing: Clean the data, handle missing values, and encode categorical variables such as merchant categories.

3. Anomaly Detection: Apply an anomaly detection model, such as an isolation forest, to identify irregular transaction patterns.

4. Model Training: Train the anomaly detection model using historical transaction data, including known fraud cases.

5. Scoring and Alerts: Assign anomaly scores to transactions, and set a threshold for triggering alerts on high-risk transactions.

6. Model Evaluation: Evaluate the model's performance using metrics like precision, recall, and the F1 score. Adjust the threshold to balance between false positives and false negatives.

7. Deployment: Integrate the trained credit card fraud detection model into Power BI, providing real-time monitoring and alerts to identify potential fraud.

Conclusion

Fraud detection and prevention are essential for safeguarding financial assets and ensuring trust in financial transactions. By understanding the key concepts and following the steps outlined above, you can successfully implement fraud detection and prevention systems in Power BI. These systems empower organizations to monitor transactions, detect anomalies, and take proactive measures to prevent fraudulent activities.

6.3 Artificial Intelligence and Natural Language Processing (NLP)

Sentiment Analysis for Market Trends

Sentiment analysis is a powerful technique that allows finance professionals to gauge public sentiment and opinions about financial markets, stocks, or assets by analyzing textual data from sources like news articles, social media, and financial reports. In this section, we will delve into the specifics of sentiment analysis for market trends using Power BI, offering a step-by-step guide, real-world examples, and insights into the value of this analysis.

Understanding Sentiment Analysis for Market Trends

Sentiment analysis, also known as opinion mining, involves determining the sentiment or emotion expressed in a piece of text, typically categorized as positive, negative, or neutral. In the context of finance, sentiment analysis is used to gauge market sentiment, which can impact investment decisions, stock prices, and market trends.

Key Components of Sentiment Analysis

1. Text Data: Sentiment analysis relies on textual data, such as news articles, social media posts, and financial reports.

2. Sentiment Scoring: Sentiment analysis models assign a numerical score to each piece of text, indicating its sentiment. For example, a positive score for a news article might indicate bullish sentiment about a particular stock.

3. Data Sources: Data sources for sentiment analysis can include financial news websites, social media platforms, and specialized financial news feeds.

4. Text Preprocessing: Text data is preprocessed to remove noise, clean the text, and handle linguistic nuances.

Steps to Implement Sentiment Analysis for Market Trends in Power BI

To conduct sentiment analysis for market trends in Power BI, follow these steps:

1. Data Collection: Gather text data from relevant sources, such as financial news articles, tweets, or other text-based sources that discuss market trends.

2. Text Preprocessing: Preprocess the text data by cleaning and removing noise, including punctuation, stop words, and special characters.

3. Sentiment Analysis Model: Use a pre-trained sentiment analysis model or build your own model. Such models can be rule-based, lexicon-based, or machine learning-based.

4. Sentiment Scoring: Apply the sentiment analysis model to the text data to assign sentiment scores (positive, negative, or neutral) to each piece of text.

5. Data Integration: Integrate the sentiment scores into your Power BI reports or dashboards to monitor market sentiment.

6. Visualization: Create visualizations, such as sentiment trend charts, to track changes in market sentiment over time.

7. Analysis and Insights: Analyze the sentiment trends and use insights to inform investment decisions or market predictions.

Real-world Example: Sentiment Analysis of Financial News

Let's illustrate the steps with a real-world example of sentiment analysis of financial news using Power BI:

1. Data Collection: Collect financial news articles from sources like Bloomberg, Reuters, and financial news APIs.

2. Text Preprocessing: Clean the text data by removing punctuation, stop words, and special characters.

3. Sentiment Analysis Model: Utilize a pre-trained sentiment analysis model or build a custom model using machine learning techniques.

4. Sentiment Scoring: Apply the sentiment analysis model to the financial news articles to assign sentiment scores (positive, negative, or neutral).

5. Data Integration: Integrate the sentiment scores into Power BI reports or dashboards to track market sentiment.

6. Visualization: Create line charts or sentiment trend visualizations to monitor changes in market sentiment over time.

7. Analysis and Insights: Analyze the sentiment trends to make informed investment decisions or predict market movements.

Conclusion

Sentiment analysis for market trends is a valuable tool for finance professionals to gain insights into market sentiment and public opinion. By following the steps outlined above and integrating sentiment analysis into Power BI, organizations can monitor market sentiment in real-time, potentially improving investment decisions and market predictions.

AI-Driven Chatbots for Financial Services

Artificial Intelligence (AI)-driven chatbots are revolutionizing the way financial services interact with customers and clients. These intelligent virtual assistants are capable of providing a wide range of services, from answering customer inquiries to executing financial transactions. In this section, we will explore the use of AI-driven chatbots in the financial sector, provide concrete examples, and offer a step-by-step guide to building your own chatbot for financial services using Power BI.

Understanding AI-Driven Chatbots for Financial Services

AI-driven chatbots are software applications powered by natural language processing (NLP) and machine learning algorithms. They can understand and respond to user queries in a human-like manner. In the financial services industry, chatbots have become invaluable for a variety of tasks, including customer support, account management, and financial advisory.

Key Features of AI-Driven Chatbots

1. Natural Language Processing (NLP): Chatbots use NLP to understand and interpret user text or speech inputs.

2. Machine Learning: Machine learning models within chatbots enable them to learn and improve their responses over time.

3. Seamless Integration: Chatbots can be integrated into various communication channels, such as websites, mobile apps, and messaging platforms.

4. 24/7 Availability: Chatbots are available around the clock, providing immediate responses to customer queries.

Steps to Build an AI-Driven Chatbot for Financial Services in Power BI

To create an AI-driven chatbot for financial services in Power BI, follow these steps:

1. Define Objectives: Clearly define the objectives and tasks you want the chatbot to perform, such as answering frequently asked questions, providing account information, or executing transactions.

2. Data Collection: Gather historical customer inquiries and responses to train your chatbot.

3. NLP Model Selection: Choose or build a natural language processing model to understand and interpret user queries.

4. Machine Learning: Train your chatbot using machine learning algorithms. You can use pre-built NLP models or create custom models.

5. Integration: Integrate your chatbot into the desired communication channels, such as your website, mobile app, or messaging platforms.

6. Testing and Fine-tuning: Test your chatbot with real users and gather feedback for improvements. Fine-tune the chatbot's responses.

7. Security and Compliance: Ensure that your chatbot adheres to data security and privacy regulations, especially in the financial sector.

8. Continuous Improvement: Continuously monitor and improve your chatbot's performance by analyzing user interactions and feedback.

Real-world Example: Customer Support Chatbot

Let's explore a real-world example of an AI-driven chatbot designed for customer support in the financial sector:

1. Define Objectives: The primary objective of the chatbot is to provide quick and accurate responses to customer inquiries related to account balances, transaction history, and account management.

2. Data Collection: Gather historical customer inquiries and responses from existing customer support interactions.

3. NLP Model Selection: Choose a pre-built NLP model that excels in understanding financial terminology and customer inquiries.

4. Machine Learning: Train the chatbot using machine learning to improve its accuracy and responsiveness.

5. Integration: Integrate the chatbot into the financial institution's website and mobile app, allowing customers to access support 24/7.

6. Testing and Fine-tuning: Test the chatbot with real customers and collect feedback to fine-tune its responses. Refine its knowledge base over time.

7. Security and Compliance: Ensure the chatbot complies with data security and privacy regulations, such as GDPR or HIPAA.

8. Continuous Improvement: Continuously monitor and improve the chatbot's performance based on user interactions and feedback.

Conclusion

AI-driven chatbots are transforming customer interactions in the financial services industry, enhancing user experience, and increasing operational efficiency. By following the steps outlined above and integrating an AI-driven chatbot into Power BI, financial organizations can offer responsive and efficient customer support, account management, and financial advisory services, ultimately improving customer satisfaction and loyalty.

Text Analytics in Financial Reporting

Text analytics is a powerful technique in the world of finance and accounting that involves extracting valuable insights from unstructured textual data, such as financial reports, earnings call transcripts, news articles, and more. In this section, we will explore the application of text analytics in financial reporting using Power BI, providing a step-by-step guide, real-world examples, and the value it brings to financial analysis.

Understanding Text Analytics in Financial Reporting

Text analytics, also known as text mining or natural language processing (NLP), enables financial professionals to process and analyze textual data for valuable insights. This unstructured data can contain essential information about market trends, sentiment, and events that impact financial decision-making.

Key Components of Text Analytics

1. Data Sources: Text data for financial reporting can be sourced from annual reports, earnings call transcripts, news articles, social media, and other textual sources.

2. Text Preprocessing: Preprocess text data to remove noise, perform tokenization, handle linguistic nuances, and apply techniques such as stemming and lemmatization.

3. Sentiment Analysis: Determine the sentiment conveyed in the text, which can provide insights into market sentiment and public opinion about financial events.

4. Keyword Extraction: Identify and extract keywords or key phrases that are relevant to financial analysis and reporting.

Steps to Implement Text Analytics in Financial Reporting with Power BI

To leverage text analytics in financial reporting using Power BI, follow these steps:

1. Data Collection: Gather the unstructured textual data from relevant sources, such as earnings call transcripts or news articles.

2. Text Preprocessing: Clean and preprocess the text data, including removing stop words, punctuation, and special characters.

3. Sentiment Analysis: Use sentiment analysis models to determine the sentiment of the text, whether it's positive, negative, or neutral. This provides insights into market sentiment.

4. Keyword Extraction: Identify and extract keywords or key phrases that are relevant to financial analysis and reporting. These can include financial terms, company names, or event-specific keywords.

5. Text Visualization: Create visualizations, such as word clouds, bar charts, or sentiment trend charts, to present the insights from the text data in an easily understandable format.

6. Integration: Integrate the text analytics results into your financial reports and dashboards in Power BI.

7. Analysis and Insights: Analyze the text analytics results to uncover trends, patterns, or sentiments that are relevant to your financial reporting and analysis.

Real-world Example: Earnings Call Transcript Analysis

Let's illustrate text analytics in financial reporting with a real-world example of analyzing earnings call transcripts:

1. Data Collection: Collect earnings call transcripts from public companies' investor relations websites or financial news sources.

2. Text Preprocessing: Clean the text data by removing punctuation, stop words, and special characters. Perform stemming to reduce words to their base form.

3. Sentiment Analysis: Utilize a pre-trained sentiment analysis model to determine the sentiment of the transcripts, providing insights into the sentiment of the company's performance.

4. Keyword Extraction: Extract relevant financial keywords, such as revenue, profit, or growth, to focus on critical financial metrics.

5. Text Visualization: Create word clouds to visualize the most frequently mentioned terms in the transcripts. Build sentiment trend charts to track sentiment changes over time.

6. Integration: Integrate the results into Power BI reports and dashboards, allowing financial analysts to access textual insights alongside financial data.

7. Analysis and Insights: Analyze the sentiment, keyword frequency, and other text analytics results to gain a deeper understanding of the company's financial performance and outlook.

Conclusion

Text analytics in financial reporting offers a valuable way to extract insights from unstructured textual data, enhancing the depth of financial analysis and reporting. By following the steps outlined above and integrating text analytics into Power BI, finance professionals can gain a more comprehensive view of financial events and market sentiment, ultimately making more informed decisions and delivering richer financial reports.

6.4 Future Trends in Financial Analytics

Blockchain and Cryptocurrency Analysis

Blockchain technology and cryptocurrencies have transformed the financial landscape, offering new opportunities and challenges for finance and accounting professionals. In this section, we will explore how Power BI can be used for blockchain and cryptocurrency analysis. We'll provide a detailed guide, real-world examples, and insights into harnessing the power of these technologies for financial insights.

Understanding Blockchain and Cryptocurrency Analysis

Blockchain is a decentralized ledger technology that underpins cryptocurrencies like Bitcoin and Ethereum. It records transactions in a secure, transparent, and immutable manner. Cryptocurrency analysis involves monitoring and analyzing cryptocurrency markets, transactions, and performance.

Key Aspects of Blockchain and Cryptocurrency Analysis

1. Blockchain Explorer Data: Data for cryptocurrency analysis is often obtained from blockchain explorers, which provide transaction history, addresses, and blocks.

2. Price and Market Data: Monitoring cryptocurrency prices, trading volumes, and market data is crucial for analysis.

3. Transaction Analysis: Studying cryptocurrency transactions can reveal trends, such as wallet movements, large transactions, and more.

4. Sentiment Analysis: Understanding the sentiment in cryptocurrency communities and news is essential for predicting market movements.

Steps to Implement Blockchain and Cryptocurrency Analysis with Power BI

To perform blockchain and cryptocurrency analysis in Power BI, follow these steps:

1. Data Collection: Gather blockchain data from blockchain explorers, cryptocurrency exchange APIs, or other relevant sources.

2. Data Cleaning: Clean and preprocess the data to remove inconsistencies and prepare it for analysis.

3. Price and Market Data: Collect and integrate real-time cryptocurrency price and market data into Power BI.

4. Transaction Analysis: Analyze transaction data to identify trends, wallet movements, and large transactions.

5. Sentiment Analysis: Implement sentiment analysis models to gauge the sentiment of cryptocurrency communities and news.

6. Visualization: Create visualizations, such as candlestick charts, line charts, and sentiment analysis dashboards, to monitor and understand cryptocurrency performance.

7. Predictive Modeling: Implement predictive models to forecast cryptocurrency prices or analyze market trends.

8. Security: Ensure the security of cryptocurrency data, especially if handling large amounts of value.

Real-world Example: Cryptocurrency Portfolio Analysis

Let's illustrate blockchain and cryptocurrency analysis with a real-world example of a cryptocurrency portfolio analysis:

1. Data Collection: Gather data from blockchain explorers and cryptocurrency exchanges to obtain transaction history, wallet addresses, and cryptocurrency balances.

2. Data Cleaning: Clean and preprocess the data to handle missing values and ensure data integrity.

3. Price and Market Data: Integrate real-time cryptocurrency price and market data from multiple exchanges to monitor portfolio performance.

4. Transaction Analysis: Analyze transaction data to track cryptocurrency movements, portfolio diversification, and trading performance.

5. Sentiment Analysis: Implement sentiment analysis models to track the sentiment in cryptocurrency communities and news.

6. Visualization: Create a Power BI dashboard with visualizations that show portfolio value over time, asset allocation, and sentiment trends.

7. Predictive Modeling: Implement predictive models to forecast cryptocurrency prices and optimize portfolio allocation.

8. Security: Ensure the security of the portfolio and consider using hardware wallets or secure storage methods for cryptocurrencies.

Conclusion

Blockchain and cryptocurrency analysis with Power BI is an exciting frontier in finance and accounting. By following the steps outlined above and integrating blockchain data and cryptocurrency market data into Power BI, finance professionals can gain valuable insights into cryptocurrency portfolio performance, market trends, and sentiment. These insights can inform investment decisions and provide a deeper understanding of this evolving financial landscape.

Integrating IoT Data for Financial Insights

The integration of Internet of Things (IoT) data into financial analytics is becoming increasingly important for finance and accounting professionals. IoT devices generate vast amounts of data that can provide valuable insights for financial decision-making. In this section, we will explore how Power BI can be used to integrate and analyze IoT data to unlock financial insights. We will provide a detailed guide, real-world examples, and a step-by-step approach to leveraging IoT data for financial analysis.

Understanding IoT Data in Financial Analytics

IoT refers to the network of interconnected devices and sensors that collect and exchange data. These devices can include anything from sensors in manufacturing equipment to smart meters in utilities. When utilized in financial analytics, IoT data can offer insights into various aspects of an organization's operations, enabling cost savings, process optimization, and improved financial performance.

Key Aspects of IoT Data in Financial Analytics

1. Data Sources: IoT devices and sensors are the primary sources of IoT data. They collect data related to equipment status, usage patterns, environmental conditions, and more.

2. Real-time Data: IoT data is often generated in real-time, providing immediate insights into operations.

3. Data Variety: IoT data can be structured, semi-structured, or unstructured, and it may include text, numerical values, images, or video.

4. Data Volume: IoT devices generate massive amounts of data, making efficient data storage and analysis crucial.

Steps to Integrate IoT Data for Financial Insights with Power BI

To leverage IoT data for financial insights using Power BI, follow these steps:

1. IoT Data Collection: Deploy and configure IoT devices and sensors to collect relevant data from your organization's operations.

2. Data Ingestion: Ingest the IoT data into a data storage solution, such as a data lake or cloud-based storage.

3. Data Cleaning and Transformation: Clean, preprocess, and transform the IoT data to make it suitable for analysis. This may involve removing noise, handling missing values, and converting data types.

4. Data Integration: Combine IoT data with financial data and other relevant data sources, creating a unified data repository.

5. Data Visualization: Develop Power BI dashboards and reports to visualize the integrated data, providing insights into operations and their financial impact.

6. Analysis and Insights: Use Power BI to analyze the integrated IoT data and financial data, uncovering trends, patterns, and correlations that impact financial performance.

7. Predictive Analytics: Implement predictive models to forecast financial outcomes and identify potential cost-saving opportunities.

8. Actionable Insights: Translate insights into actionable recommendations for financial decision-making and process optimization.

Real-world Example: Manufacturing Process Optimization

Let's explore a real-world example of integrating IoT data for financial insights in the manufacturing industry:

1. IoT Data Collection: Deploy IoT sensors on manufacturing equipment to monitor machine performance, temperature, and energy consumption.

2. Data Ingestion: Ingest IoT data into a cloud-based data storage system, where it can be easily accessed.

3. Data Cleaning and Transformation: Clean and preprocess the data to remove outliers and correct measurement errors.

4. Data Integration: Combine IoT data with financial data, such as production costs and maintenance expenses, creating a unified data repository.

5. Data Visualization: Develop Power BI dashboards that provide real-time insights into machine performance, energy usage, and their impact on production costs.

6. Analysis and Insights: Analyze the integrated data to identify correlations between machine performance and financial outcomes. Discover opportunities to optimize processes and reduce costs.

7. Predictive Analytics: Implement predictive models to forecast machine failures and production disruptions, allowing for proactive maintenance and cost reduction.

8. Actionable Insights: Translate insights into actionable recommendations, such as adjusting maintenance schedules or upgrading equipment to improve financial performance.

Conclusion

Integrating IoT data for financial insights with Power BI offers finance and accounting professionals the opportunity to harness real-time data from IoT devices to optimize processes, reduce costs, and improve financial performance. By following the steps outlined above and creating Power BI dashboards, organizations can uncover hidden patterns and correlations, ultimately enhancing their decision-making and financial outcomes.

Quantum Computing in Finance

Quantum computing, an emerging technology with the potential to revolutionize various industries, including finance, is a fascinating topic. In this section, we will delve into how quantum computing can be harnessed in the world of finance using Power BI. We'll provide an in-depth exploration, real-world examples, and a step-by-step guide to utilizing quantum computing for financial analytics.

Understanding Quantum Computing in Finance

Quantum computing leverages the principles of quantum mechanics to perform calculations that are practically impossible for classical computers. In finance, it holds the promise of solving complex optimization problems, simulating financial models, and enhancing data security. Key areas where quantum computing can impact finance include portfolio optimization, risk management, option pricing, and fraud detection.

Key Aspects of Quantum Computing in Finance

1. Quantum Algorithms: Quantum computers are expected to bring advancements in algorithms that can solve complex financial problems more efficiently.

2. Quantum Simulations: Quantum computers can simulate financial models, helping with risk assessment and strategy development.

3. Quantum Cryptography: Quantum cryptography can enhance the security of financial transactions and data.

Steps to Utilize Quantum Computing for Financial Insights with Power BI

Although quantum computing is in its infancy and not yet widely accessible, the following steps can be considered for its integration into financial analytics using Power BI in the future:

1. Quantum Computing Infrastructure: Establish access to a quantum computing infrastructure or service.

2. Problem Formulation: Identify financial problems that could benefit from quantum computing, such as portfolio optimization, option pricing, or risk assessment.

3. Quantum Algorithm Development: Collaborate with quantum computing experts to develop quantum algorithms that address the identified financial problems.

4. Data Integration: Integrate financial data, including historical market data and portfolio information, into the quantum computing environment.

5. Quantum Simulation: Utilize quantum computing for simulations and optimizations. For example, in portfolio optimization, quantum computing can be used to find optimal asset allocations based on various constraints and risk factors.

6. Result Visualization: Develop Power BI dashboards to visualize the results and insights obtained from quantum computing simulations.

7. Implementation of Quantum Cryptography: Explore the implementation of quantum cryptography for enhanced data security in financial transactions.

Real-world Example: Portfolio Optimization with Quantum Computing

Let's illustrate how quantum computing can be used in financial analytics with a real-world example of portfolio optimization:

1. Quantum Computing Infrastructure: Access a quantum computing service, such as IBM Quantum or a similar platform.

2. Problem Formulation: Define the portfolio optimization problem, including constraints, risk factors, and return objectives.

3. Quantum Algorithm Development: Collaborate with quantum computing experts to develop a quantum algorithm that can efficiently solve the portfolio optimization problem.

4. Data Integration: Integrate historical market data, asset information, and risk models into the quantum computing environment.

5. Quantum Simulation: Utilize quantum computing to simulate various portfolio allocation scenarios, considering different constraints and risk factors.

6. Result Visualization: Create a Power BI dashboard that displays the optimal portfolio allocation, risk assessments, and historical performance.

7. Implementation of Quantum Cryptography: Explore the use of quantum cryptography to secure financial data and transactions related to portfolio management.

Conclusion

Quantum computing holds significant potential for transforming financial analytics by addressing complex problems in portfolio optimization, risk management, and data security. While quantum computing is still in its infancy, it is essential for finance and accounting professionals to stay informed about its developments and prepare for its integration with tools like Power BI. As quantum computing evolves, it will likely offer new avenues for financial insights and decision-making in the ever-changing landscape of finance.

6.5 Ethical and Regulatory Considerations

Data Privacy and Ethics in Financial Analytics

In the rapidly evolving landscape of finance, where data is at the heart of decision-making, maintaining data privacy and adhering to ethical standards are of paramount importance. In this section, we will explore the crucial aspects of data privacy and ethics in financial analytics, with a focus on using Power BI. We will provide an in-depth discussion, practical examples, and a step-by-step guide on how to ensure data privacy and ethical practices in financial analytics.

Understanding Data Privacy and Ethics in Financial Analytics

Financial analytics involves handling sensitive and often confidential data. It's essential to strike a balance between leveraging data for insights and ensuring the privacy and ethical use of that data. Here are key aspects to consider:

Data Privacy

1. Confidentiality: Financial data often contains sensitive information about individuals and organizations. Protecting this data from unauthorized access is a fundamental requirement.

2. Data Encryption: Utilize encryption techniques to secure data both in transit and at rest. Ensure that data is unreadable to unauthorized users.

3. Access Control: Implement access controls and authentication mechanisms to restrict data access to authorized personnel only.

4. Compliance: Adhere to data protection regulations such as GDPR (General Data Protection Regulation) and HIPAA (Health Insurance Portability and Accountability Act) when handling personal and financial data.

Ethics

1. Fair Use: Ensure that data is used in a fair and unbiased manner. Avoid discriminatory practices that may result from data analytics.

2. Transparency: Be transparent about the data you collect, how it's used, and the decisions made based on the data.

3. Accountability: Establish accountability within the organization for ethical data practices. Designate individuals responsible for ensuring data ethics.

4. Bias Mitigation: Implement techniques to identify and mitigate biases in data and algorithms to prevent unintended consequences.

Steps to Ensure Data Privacy and Ethics in Financial Analytics with Power BI

To maintain data privacy and uphold ethical standards in financial analytics using Power BI, follow these steps:

1. Data Classification: Identify and classify the data used in financial analytics. Distinguish between public, sensitive, and confidential data.

2. Compliance Assessment: Evaluate your financial analytics practices against relevant data protection regulations, such as GDPR or HIPAA, to ensure compliance.

3. Data Anonymization: If applicable, anonymize or pseudonymize sensitive data to protect individual identities while retaining data utility.

4. Ethical Framework Development: Create an ethical framework or policy that outlines guidelines for data usage, analytics, and decision-making.

5. Ethical Review: Prior to deploying financial analytics solutions, conduct an ethical review of algorithms, data sources, and potential biases.

6. Transparency Measures: Enhance transparency by providing clear explanations of data sources, analytical methods, and the implications of financial decisions.

7. Bias Detection and Mitigation: Implement tools and techniques to detect and mitigate biases in data and algorithms.

8. Ethical Training: Provide training to personnel involved in financial analytics, emphasizing the importance of data ethics and privacy.

Real-world Example: Ethical Data Usage in Credit Scoring

Let's consider a real-world example in credit scoring, where data privacy and ethics are critical:

1. Data Classification: Classify credit applicant data as sensitive. This data contains personal and financial information.

2. Compliance Assessment: Evaluate credit scoring practices against relevant regulations, such as the Equal Credit Opportunity Act (ECOA) in the U.S., to ensure fair lending practices.

3. Data Anonymization: Anonymize personal information in credit applicant data to protect individual identities while retaining data utility for scoring.

4. Ethical Framework Development: Develop an ethical framework that outlines guidelines for fair credit scoring and bias mitigation.

5. Ethical Review: Before deploying the credit scoring model, conduct an ethical review to detect and mitigate biases that could result in unfair lending practices.

6. Transparency Measures: Provide loan applicants with clear explanations of the factors used in their credit score and how those factors influence lending decisions.

7. Bias Detection and Mitigation: Implement techniques to detect and mitigate biases related to factors like race, gender, or age in the credit scoring model.

8. Ethical Training: Train credit analysts and data scientists on the importance of ethical data usage and fair lending practices.

Conclusion

Data privacy and ethical considerations are integral to maintaining trust and credibility in financial analytics. Using Power BI, finance and accounting professionals can ensure that data privacy regulations are met, ethical data practices are followed, and that financial decisions are made without discrimination or bias. By following the steps outlined above, organizations can build a foundation of trust with their stakeholders and contribute to a more ethical and responsible financial ecosystem.

Compliance with Evolving Financial Regulations

In the ever-changing landscape of finance and accounting, staying compliant with evolving financial regulations is crucial for organizations using Power BI for their analytics and reporting needs. This section will delve into the nuances of compliance, offering a comprehensive guide to ensure that your financial analytics remain aligned with the latest regulatory standards. We will provide real-world examples, step-by-step instructions, and, where relevant, code illustrations to help you navigate this complex landscape.

The Importance of Compliance

Compliance with financial regulations is not only a legal requirement but also a means of ensuring financial stability, transparency, and trust in the industry. Various regulations exist to protect investors, prevent financial crimes, and maintain the integrity of financial data. Ignoring compliance can result in legal troubles, reputational damage, and financial losses.

Key Financial Regulations

To maintain compliance, you must be familiar with key financial regulations that may affect your organization. These can include:

1. Sarbanes-Oxley Act (SOX): Regulates financial reporting to protect investors from fraudulent accounting activities.

2. General Data Protection Regulation (GDPR): Ensures the protection of personal data and privacy for individuals within the European Union.

3. The Dodd-Frank Wall Street Reform and Consumer Protection Act: Addresses financial market stability and consumer protection.

4. The Basel III Accords: Focuses on bank capital adequacy, stress testing, and market risk.

5. Financial Accounting Standards Board (FASB) Standards: Governs accounting standards in the United States.

6. International Financial Reporting Standards (IFRS): Sets international accounting standards.

Steps to Ensure Compliance with Financial Regulations Using Power BI

Compliance is an ongoing process. To ensure that your financial analytics using Power BI remain compliant with evolving financial regulations, follow these steps:

1. Regulation Assessment: Regularly assess which financial regulations apply to your organization based on your location, industry, and the nature of your operations.

2. Data Classification: Classify your financial data into categories based on their sensitivity and compliance requirements.

3. Data Governance Framework: Develop a robust data governance framework to manage data quality, accuracy, and security.

4. Documentation: Maintain comprehensive documentation of your data sources, processes, and reports, including any changes made.

5. Security and Access Controls: Implement security measures and access controls to ensure only authorized personnel can view or modify financial data.

6. Regular Audits and Testing: Conduct regular internal audits and testing to identify any compliance issues and rectify them promptly.

7. Regulatory Reporting: Use Power BI to generate reports that comply with the specific requirements of financial regulations. Ensure reports are accurate, transparent, and easily auditable.

8. Training and Awareness: Provide training to employees on compliance requirements, and foster a culture of compliance within the organization.

Real-world Example: SOX Compliance with Power BI

Consider a scenario where your organization needs to comply with the Sarbanes-Oxley Act (SOX), which requires accurate financial reporting and internal controls. Here's how Power BI can assist in SOX compliance:

1. Regulation Assessment: Identify the sections of SOX relevant to your organization's financial reporting processes.

2. Data Classification: Classify financial data into categories based on their importance for SOX compliance.

3. Data Governance Framework: Implement data governance measures to ensure data quality, consistency, and integrity.

4. Documentation: Maintain documentation of data sources, transformations, and the report creation process.

5. Security and Access Controls: Use Power BI's role-based security to restrict access to sensitive financial data.

6. Regular Audits and Testing: Schedule regular audits of your Power BI reports and conduct SOX compliance testing.

7. Regulatory Reporting: Create SOX compliance reports using Power BI, ensuring they meet SOX requirements for accuracy and transparency.

8. Training and Awareness: Train employees involved in financial reporting on SOX compliance, making them aware of their responsibilities.

Conclusion

Compliance with evolving financial regulations is an ongoing commitment that requires careful planning, documentation, and the right tools, such as Power BI. By following these steps and staying proactive in adapting to new regulatory changes, your organization can confidently navigate the complex landscape of financial compliance, ensuring that financial data remains accurate, transparent, and trustworthy. This not only helps in avoiding legal complications but also builds trust and credibility with stakeholders.

6.6 Case Studies and Success Stories

Real-world Applications of Advanced Analytics in Finance

In this section, we will explore real-world applications of advanced analytics in the field of finance using Power BI. The power of advanced analytics goes beyond traditional reporting and visualization, enabling finance professionals to gain deeper insights, make informed decisions, and drive business growth. We will provide specific examples, step-by-step guidance, and, when applicable, code illustrations to illustrate the practical implementation of advanced analytics in finance.

Enhancing Financial Forecasting

One of the primary applications of advanced analytics in finance is enhancing financial forecasting. By using historical financial data and applying advanced analytics techniques, organizations can make more accurate predictions about future financial performance. Let's consider an example:

Scenario: A retail company wants to improve its sales forecasting. They have historical sales data, and they want to apply advanced analytics to create more accurate sales forecasts.

Steps:

1. Data Collection: Gather historical sales data, including information on product categories, sales channels, and past promotions.

2. Data Preparation: Clean and preprocess the data to ensure it is ready for analysis. This may involve handling missing values, outliers, and data transformation.

3. Data Exploration: Use Power BI to explore the data visually. Create visualizations such as line charts, scatter plots, and histograms to gain insights into sales trends.

4. Advanced Analytics: Apply advanced forecasting techniques in Power BI, such as time series analysis or machine learning models. Power BI provides integration with R and Python for advanced analytics.

5. Model Evaluation: Evaluate the forecasting model's performance using metrics like Mean Absolute Error (MAE) and Root Mean Squared Error (RMSE).

6. Visualization: Create interactive dashboards in Power BI that display historical sales data, actual sales, and forecasted sales. Users can interact with the data and adjust parameters to see the impact on forecasts.

7. Continuous Monitoring: Set up regular data updates and retraining of the forecasting model to ensure it remains accurate.

Fraud Detection and Prevention

Another critical application of advanced analytics in finance is fraud detection and prevention. Financial institutions and organizations can leverage advanced analytics to identify suspicious transactions and prevent fraudulent activities. Let's examine a case:

Scenario: A bank wants to improve its fraud detection system. They want to detect unusual patterns and potentially fraudulent transactions in real-time.

Steps:

1. Data Integration: Integrate transaction data, customer information, and historical fraud data into a central database.

2. Data Preprocessing: Clean and transform the data to make it suitable for analysis. This involves data normalization, feature engineering, and handling missing values.

3. Real-time Data Stream: Implement a real-time data stream into Power BI to monitor incoming transactions as they happen.

4. Advanced Analytics: Utilize machine learning algorithms, such as anomaly detection models, to identify potentially fraudulent transactions.

5. Alerting System: Set up an alerting system within Power BI to notify the fraud prevention team in real-time when suspicious transactions are detected.

6. Investigation Dashboard: Create a dedicated dashboard in Power BI that allows fraud analysts to investigate flagged transactions. This dashboard should provide transaction details, customer profiles, and historical data.

7. Feedback Loop: Implement a feedback loop where the results of investigations are used to improve the fraud detection models.

Portfolio Risk Management

Portfolio risk management is crucial in the finance industry, and advanced analytics can provide valuable insights into the risk associated with investment portfolios. Consider the following example:

Scenario: An investment firm manages a portfolio of assets and wants to assess the risk associated with the portfolio.

Steps:

1. Data Collection: Gather data on the portfolio's assets, including historical price data, financial ratios, and economic indicators.

2. Data Preprocessing: Clean and prepare the data for analysis. This may involve aligning data from different sources and dealing with missing values.

3. Risk Metrics: Calculate various risk metrics, such as Value at Risk (VaR), Conditional Value at Risk (CVaR), and beta coefficients.

4. Scenario Analysis: Use Power BI to perform scenario analysis to assess how the portfolio's value would change under different market conditions.

5. Visualization: Create interactive dashboards that display risk metrics, scenario analysis results, and historical portfolio performance. Users can explore the impact of different scenarios.

6. Sensitivity Analysis: Perform sensitivity analysis to understand how changes in input parameters affect the portfolio's risk.

7. Reporting: Generate regular risk reports for portfolio managers and clients using Power BI's reporting capabilities.

Conclusion

These real-world applications demonstrate how advanced analytics in finance, powered by Power BI, can provide valuable insights and drive better decision-making. Whether it's enhancing financial forecasting, detecting and preventing fraud, or managing portfolio risk, the capabilities of Power BI enable finance professionals to leverage data-driven insights for improved financial performance and risk management. By following these steps and adapting them to specific use cases, organizations can harness the full potential of advanced analytics in finance.

Achieving Competitive Advantage with Cutting-Edge Analytics

In this section, we'll explore how organizations can achieve a competitive advantage in the finance and accounting industry by leveraging cutting-edge analytics with Power BI. The rapid advancement of analytics tools and techniques provides opportunities for financial professionals to gain insights, improve decision-making, and outperform their competitors. We'll illustrate this with a specific example, step-by-step guidance, and, where relevant, code examples to demonstrate the implementation of cutting-edge analytics.

The Competitive Landscape in Finance

The finance and accounting industry is highly competitive. Organizations continually seek ways to gain an edge in various areas, including customer service, risk management, cost reduction, and financial performance. Cutting-edge analytics can be a game-changer in this context, offering the potential for innovative solutions and insights that competitors may not possess.

Example: Personalized Financial Planning

Scenario: A financial advisory firm aims to stand out by offering highly personalized financial planning services to its clients. Traditional financial planning tools provide generic advice, but the firm wants to create a cutting-edge, data-driven approach.

Steps:

1. Data Collection: Gather detailed data about each client, including financial goals, income, expenses, investment preferences, risk tolerance, and more.

2. Data Integration: Integrate various data sources into Power BI, such as client data, market data, and economic indicators.

3. Machine Learning Models: Utilize machine learning algorithms for financial planning. For example, use regression models to predict future investment returns or Monte Carlo simulations for risk assessment.

4. Personalized Recommendations: Develop algorithms that provide personalized financial recommendations based on each client's unique circumstances. This may include investment strategies, retirement planning, and tax optimization.

5. Visualization: Create interactive Power BI dashboards that present personalized financial plans, investment scenarios, and retirement projections. Clients can explore different options and understand the impact of their decisions.

6. Real-time Updates: Implement a system that offers real-time updates on the performance of investments, ensuring that financial plans remain aligned with clients' goals.

7. Client Engagement: Use Power BI to communicate financial plans effectively, allowing clients to engage with their personalized recommendations and make informed decisions.

8. Feedback and Adaptation: Continuously collect feedback from clients and adapt the personalized financial planning models to improve the quality of recommendations.

The Power of Cutting-Edge Analytics

By embracing cutting-edge analytics in financial planning, the advisory firm can offer a level of personalization and data-driven decision-making that sets them apart from competitors. Clients receive tailored recommendations that adapt to changing circumstances, ultimately enhancing their financial well-being and building trust in the firm's services.

Conclusion

In the competitive landscape of finance and accounting, achieving a competitive advantage through cutting-edge analytics is not just a possibility but a necessity. Organizations that leverage advanced analytics tools like Power BI can transform their services, providing more value to clients, making better decisions, and ultimately outperforming their rivals. The example of personalized financial planning showcases how data-driven approaches can lead to a distinct advantage in the industry, setting the stage for future success.

6.7 The Path Forward

Building a Roadmap for Advanced Financial Analytics with Power BI

In this section, we'll outline the process of building a roadmap for advanced financial analytics using Power BI. A well-structured roadmap is essential for organizations looking to harness the full potential of Power BI and stay ahead in the rapidly evolving landscape of financial analytics. We'll provide specific steps, practical examples, and, where applicable, code explanations to guide you through the process.

The Importance of a Roadmap

A roadmap serves as a strategic plan that outlines the key objectives, milestones, and actions required to achieve advanced financial analytics using Power BI. It helps organizations align their analytics initiatives with business goals, allocate resources efficiently, and adapt to changing market conditions.

Step 1: Define Business Goals

Begin by clearly defining your organization's business goals. These could include improving financial reporting accuracy, optimizing budgeting and forecasting, enhancing risk management, or increasing profitability. The goals should be specific, measurable, achievable, relevant, and time-bound (SMART).

Example: The business goal is to reduce operational costs by 15% within the next fiscal year.

Step 2: Identify Key Metrics

Identify the key performance indicators (KPIs) and metrics that are critical to measuring progress toward your business goals. These metrics will drive the analytics you build in Power BI.

Example: If the goal is cost reduction, key metrics might include cost per unit, cost variance, and cost-to-revenue ratio.

Step 3: Data Assessment

Evaluate your existing data infrastructure. Assess the quality, availability, and relevance of your data sources. Identify any gaps that need to be addressed to support your analytics initiatives.

Example: You find that your data sources for cost data are fragmented and lack real-time updates. This will be a focus for improvement.

Step 4: Tool Selection

Choose the Power BI tools and licenses that align with your organization's needs and budget. Decide whether to use Power BI Desktop, Power BI Pro, or Power BI Premium, considering factors like user collaboration and data volume.

Example: Based on your data assessment, you choose Power BI Premium to handle large datasets and real-time data updates.

Step 5: Data Preparation

Prepare your data for analysis in Power BI. This may involve data cleansing, transformation, and modeling to ensure it's ready for building reports and dashboards.

Example: You clean and model your cost data, creating relationships and measures to calculate the key metrics identified.

Step 6: Report and Dashboard Development

Leverage Power BI to create reports and dashboards that visualize your key metrics and KPIs. Ensure that the visualizations provide actionable insights and are user-friendly.

Example: You build a cost dashboard with visualizations showing cost trends, cost breakdowns, and comparisons to previous periods.

Step 7: Testing and Validation

Thoroughly test the reports and dashboards to validate the accuracy of the analytics. Involve key stakeholders to review and provide feedback.

Example: Your finance team validates the cost reduction analytics and provides feedback, which leads to further improvements.

Step 8: Deployment and User Training

Deploy the Power BI reports and dashboards to your finance team. Provide training and resources to ensure they can effectively use the tools for decision-making.

Example: You conduct training sessions to familiarize the finance team with the cost reduction dashboard and its features.

Step 9: Monitor and Iterate

Continuously monitor the performance of your analytics, track the progress of your business goals, and iterate on your reports and dashboards as needed.

Example: You regularly review cost reduction progress and make adjustments to the dashboard to reflect changing circumstances.

Conclusion

Building a roadmap for advanced financial analytics with Power BI is a strategic process that ensures alignment with business objectives and efficient use of resources. By following the steps outlined and continuously iterating on your analytics, you can leverage Power BI to drive informed financial decisions and gain a competitive edge in the finance and accounting field.

Developing Skills and Talent for Future-Ready Finance Teams

In this section, we'll discuss the importance of developing skills and talent within finance teams to ensure they are well-prepared for the future of financial analytics with Power BI. We'll provide specific strategies and actionable steps to empower your team and maximize their effectiveness.

The Evolving Landscape of Financial Analytics

The field of financial analytics is constantly evolving, driven by technological advancements, regulatory changes, and the increasing importance of data-driven decision-making. As the landscape changes, finance teams must adapt and acquire new skills to stay competitive.

Step 1: Identify Skill Gaps

Begin by identifying the current skill levels of your finance team and understanding the skills needed to excel in the evolving financial analytics landscape. This assessment will help you pinpoint skill gaps that need to be addressed.

Example: You find that your team lacks skills in data visualization, advanced data modeling, and data storytelling.

Step 2: Create a Training Plan

Develop a comprehensive training plan that outlines the specific skills and knowledge areas your team needs to acquire. Consider a combination of in-house training, external courses, workshops, and online resources.

Example: Your training plan includes courses on advanced Power BI features, data visualization best practices, and financial data modeling.

Step 3: Hands-On Experience

Provide opportunities for hands-on experience and practical application of skills. Encourage your team to work on real financial projects that involve using Power BI for analytics.

Example: Assign team members to work on a project that involves building a financial dashboard in Power BI to analyze quarterly revenue and expenses.

Step 4: Mentorship and Collaboration

Promote mentorship and collaboration within your finance team. Experienced team members can mentor those who are developing new skills, fostering a culture of continuous learning.

Example: Senior analysts mentor junior team members in the best practices of data visualization and how to effectively communicate financial insights.

Step 5: Evaluate Progress

Regularly evaluate the progress of your team's skill development. Use assessments, feedback, and performance metrics to gauge how well they are adapting to the new skills.

Example: Conduct quarterly skill assessments and performance reviews to track skill improvements and identify areas where additional training is required.

Step 6: Stay Informed

Stay informed about the latest developments in the field of financial analytics and Power BI. Encourage your team to attend industry conferences, webinars, and seminars to stay updated.

Example: You and your team attend a finance analytics conference where you learn about the latest trends and best practices in data analysis and visualization.

Step 7: Certifications

Consider encouraging your team to pursue relevant certifications in financial analytics and Power BI. Certifications can validate their skills and enhance their professional credibility.

Example: Your team members obtain Microsoft Power BI certifications, demonstrating their proficiency in using the tool for advanced financial analytics.

Step 8: Learning Culture

Foster a learning culture within your finance team, where continuous skill development is not just a requirement but a shared value. Encourage team members to share knowledge and resources.

Example: You create a shared knowledge repository where team members can access learning materials and share their own insights and resources.

Conclusion

Developing skills and talent within your finance team is essential for creating future-ready finance teams capable of harnessing the power of Power BI for advanced financial analytics. By following these steps and nurturing a culture of continuous learning, you can ensure that your team remains agile and well-prepared for the evolving landscape of financial analytics.

CONCLUSION

In the world of finance and accounting, data is king, and Power BI has emerged as a powerful tool that unlocks valuable financial insights. Throughout this book, "Power BI for Finance and Accounting: Unlocking Financial Insights," we've embarked on a comprehensive journey, delving into the intricacies of Power BI and its applications in the finance industry.

From the fundamentals of financial reporting to advanced analytics and future trends, we've covered a wide spectrum of topics to empower finance professionals with the knowledge and skills needed to excel in their roles. We've explored the art of creating compelling financial dashboards, mastering DAX formulas, and leveraging the potential of Power BI for regulatory compliance, audit reporting, predictive analytics, and much more.

The financial world is rapidly evolving, and the ability to harness data for strategic decision-making is no longer optional—it's imperative. The extensive case studies and practical examples provided in this book should serve as a springboard for finance and accounting professionals to apply these concepts in their own organizations. The insights gained through the pages of this book can help in optimizing financial processes, improving forecasting accuracy, and achieving a deeper understanding of financial data.

We would like to express our sincere gratitude to our readers for choosing "Power BI for Finance and Accounting: Unlocking Financial Insights" as a valuable resource. Your dedication to learning and improving your financial analytics skills is commendable.

We hope that this book has been instrumental in enhancing your understanding of Power BI and its applications in the world of finance. Your pursuit of knowledge and excellence in the field is an inspiration to us.

We also want to acknowledge the hard work and dedication of the entire team that contributed to the creation of this book, from the authors to the editors and everyone in between. Writing a book is a collaborative effort, and we are proud to have had the opportunity to share our knowledge with you.

As you continue your journey in the world of finance and accounting, remember that learning is a lifelong endeavor. Stay curious, stay motivated, and never stop seeking ways to improve your skills and understanding. The world of financial analytics is rich with opportunities, and you are well-equipped to navigate it with confidence.

If you have any questions, feedback, or require further assistance, please don't hesitate to reach out. We are here to support your quest for financial insights and success.

Thank you, and best wishes for your future endeavors in the dynamic realm of finance and accounting!

Sincerely,

Made in the USA
Las Vegas, NV
06 November 2023

80355547R00114